# Discoveries

## Two Centuries of
## Poems by Mormon Women

# Discoveries

## Two Centuries of Poems by Mormon Women

Compiled and Edited by

*Susan Elizabeth Howe and Sheree Maxwell Bench*

Joseph Fielding Smith Institute for Latter-day Saint History
at Brigham Young University
Provo, Utah

Association for Mormon Letters
Provo, Utah

To my husband, Cless Young,

a great supporter of Mormon women.

——SEH




To my mother, Joan,

a Mormon woman of faith and courage.

——SMB

## Poetry

A rainbow with the hues of feeling lit;
    The opal's heart of snow and fire wrought;
Rayed with the purest light which souls emit—
    The heavenly halo which transfigures thought.

                *—Josephine Spencer*

# Contents

## Reaching

## First Bliss

## A Child of My Body

## Devotional

## Release

❧ designates poems in the dramatic performance.

# Illustrations

# Introduction

The initial impetus for this book was the 200th anniversary of the birth of renowned poet and leader of Latter-day Saint women, Eliza R. Snow. In commemoration, the Women's History Initiative team of Brigham Young University's Joseph Fielding Smith Institute for Latter-day Saint History launched a series of events focusing on Mormon women. Smith Institute director Jill Mulvay Derr suggested that a reader's theater of Mormon women's poetry from the nineteenth and twentieth centuries would complement the team's lecture series and library exhibition, which opened on Snow's birthday, January 21, 2004. Derr invited us to select and organize the poetry, and we responded with enthusiasm. The reader's theater evolved into a performance that combines dramatic interpretations of some of the poems by actresses under the direction of Char Nelson and musical interpretations of others by singers under the direction of Gayle G. Lockwood. Original music was written for the production by a fine British composer, Harriet Petherick Bushman. The first performance was held March 20, 2004, in the auditorium of the Harold B. Lee Library at Brigham Young University. Because all the excellent poems we discovered could not fit into the performance, Smith Institute faculty suggested that we publish a slightly larger collection, which is presented here.

This volume does not pretend to represent the full variety and extent of poetry written by Mormon women for the past two hundred years, so we want to clarify the principles used in selecting the poems. First, we chose poems that revealed the life experiences of a Mormon woman from her birth to her death and entrance into eternity. We chose personal poems. We chose poems that lent themselves to dramatic presentation—poems with a narrative aspect, with humor, or with vivid sensory imagery—because they had to be acted out before an audience. Finally, we chose poems that were available to us in historical archives, Latter-day Saint periodicals from both past and present, anthologies such as *Harvest: Contemporary Mormon Poems* and *A Believing People: Literature of the Latter-day Saints,* and collections we owned or could obtain. But the limitations of our selection are obvious—many fine meditative poems could not be included; nor could we include excellent poems about subjects outside the parameters of our project. We imagine and hope that there are many accomplished Latter-day Saint women poets we know nothing about, particularly young poets and international poets, who will rise to prominence in the future. Despite its limitations, this collection does show how from its beginnings in nineteenth-century Mormondom, poetry has come into its own as an art form in Latter-day Saint culture.

We also include in this volume selected images and poems from a book entitled *Songs and Flowers of the Wasatch;* this book, edited by Emmeline B. Wells, was created for display at the 1893 World's Columbian Exposition held in Chicago, Illinois, as an example of the level of refinement and education nineteenth-century Mormon women had achieved. An important work of art and literature, it features beautiful watercolor paintings by Edna Wells Sloan and original poems written by a cross-section of Utah's most accomplished Mormon women poets. Now the book is largely unknown, housed in the vault of L. Tom Perry Special Collections in the Harold B. Lee Library at BYU. It is a joy to bring some of the images of this unique historical treasure to a wider audience.

For those interested in the dramatic and musical presentation, we have marked the poems from the script with the ☙ symbol.

Some of the lengthier poems were shortened for dramatic effect. These were abridged for the performance, the standard line of periods and spaces indicating where sections have been cut; however, we were careful to preserve authorial intent as completely as possible when making these editorial decisions. Readers may refer to the bibliography for sources should they wish to locate the entire poem. It is our hope that this collection of poetry, in conjunction with the dramatic performance, has contributed to the Smith Institute's 2004 celebration of Mormon women past and present.

## Discussion of Mormon Women's Poetry

> . . . I have been writing something
> Which will likely enough be read
> By our children's children
> After we all are dead,
> And must I think I should have been
> Washing dishes instead?

This stanza from Lula Greene Richards's "An Apology," reprinted herein, aptly expresses the sentiments of Mormon women over two centuries who have determinedly found time amidst busy schedules and pressing obligations to express themselves in poetry. Readers may be surprised to learn that scores of files bulging with the writings of Mormon women hang in tall, tan filing cabinets in the Smith Institute. The names of the writers, once so familiar, now go unrecognized. Their poetry lies waiting for someone to carefully read, reflect upon, and offer scholarly analysis of creative works that convey so much about the authors' lives, concerns, and experiences.

Two collections have laid the groundwork for recovering Mormon women's poetry, and ever so slowly scholars are beginning to give these writings the careful consideration they deserve. The Relief Society's centennial anthology of verse, appropriately titled *Our Legacy* (1941), is an early compilation of poetry by Latter-day Saint women. It includes every winning entry from the Eliza R. Snow poetry contest from 1924 to 1942 as well as selected poems from *Woman's Exponent* and *Relief Society Magazine.* A more thorough search of *Woman's Exponent* and *Young Woman's Journal* was done in the early 1980s by historian Maureen Ursenbach Beecher and researcher Kylie N. Turley. The two women worked to gather every poem that appeared in these nineteenth- and early twentieth-century publications. The painstaking page-by-page search resulted in Beecher's 1985 overview of Mormon women's newspaper verse and a treasure trove of poetry in the files at Smith Institute.[1] In the past decade, a handful of graduate students have renewed efforts to reclaim virtually unknown writers such as Josephine Spencer, Lu Dalton, Hannah Tapfield King, and dozens of others.[2]

The single poet who has received the most scholarly attention is Eliza R. Snow. With nearly five hundred poems to her credit, she remains early Mormonism's most prolific woman of letters. Literary discourse on Snow's poetry includes Beecher's 1990 article discussing autobiographical elements and an important historical and theological study by historian Jill Mulvay Derr in 2000.[3] Certainly there are scores of other women whose poetry remains hidden or irretrievable because they never intended it to be shared. The poetry we have available to us now is largely the result of early writers' willingness to publish.

In a time when taking up the pen or setting type was increasingly within the purview of women, Mormon women became their own best advocates for literary achievement. They urged one another to write and financially supported the publication of each other's projects. From the outset, the pages of *Woman's Exponent* (1872–1914) and *Young Woman's Journal* (1889–1929) included creative works contributed by readers and later printed announcements of their new books.[4] Sarah Carmichael and Emmeline B. Wells were two of many authors encouraged by friends to publish, while supporters of Augusta Joyce Crocheron raised needed funds by selling advance subscriptions to her biographical compilation, *Representative Women of Deseret*.[5] New authors recognized the influence of Eliza R. Snow and expressed gratitude when their projects received her approval.[6] Church women's organizations promoted creative writing among their members as well. The Young Ladies' Mutual Improvement Association published the poetry of Ruth May Fox in 1923. That same year the Relief Society began its yearly poetry contest to pay tribute to former president Eliza R. Snow and to foster "poetic expression" among Latter-day Saint women.[7] These are just a few examples of the networking that cultivated literacy among the women and provided venues for their literary efforts.

Themes in early Latter-day Saint verse were similar to women's writings nationally as they touched on concerns political, social, and familial, as well as religious. They explored ideas and ideology, reflected upon milestones and minutia, and considered relationships with family, friends, and God. They called for reform, pressing for expanded opportunities for women and working to influence both the public and the policy makers. They wrote on nature and the seasons, employing images as metaphor for more serious topics. They celebrated special occasions. Other common themes included family relationships and bereavement as many women lost loved ones, particularly children. But there is one distinctive aspect that sets Mormon women's writing apart in a significant way. Clearly present is the undercurrent of strength and empowerment they found in the gospel of Jesus Christ. These women believed that the restoration of the Church and the organization of the Relief Society by Joseph Smith had ushered in a new day for women, and they wrote from this perspective.

These themes are reflected in this collection. In "Woman's Sphere," Lu Dalton challenges nineteenth-century limits on women's potential and asserts their need for education. In "The Bachelor Maid," Ruth May Fox describes the amazing contributions of single women. "An Apology," offered by Lula Greene Richards for neglecting domestic responsibilities in favor of writing poetry, demonstrates the challenge of filling multiple roles. Roles are also central to Emily Hill Woodmansee's "What Are the Fathers About?" where she reminds men that child rearing requires the participation of both parents. Sarah Carmichael's metaphor of "April Flowers" effectively conveys the pain of a woman in a troubling, perhaps abusive relationship, while Augusta Joyce Crocheron recounts the thrill of being "Betrothed." Milestones are the subjects of two poems: "A Mother's Farewell" was written by Emily Hill Woodmansee for a woman who realizes she may never see her newlywed daughter again, and Augusta Joyce Crocheron's "The Baby" expresses a mother's simultaneous joy and sadness as she contemplates the meaning of her child's first steps. In an unusual twist, "On My Fourteenth Birthday" mourns the loss of Lula Greene Richards's youth, while Ruth May Fox celebrates the life of "Our Beloved Mother Zina D. H. Young" upon her death.

The remaining poems by nineteenth-century poets deal with war, internal struggle, and the peace of the gospel on a personal level. "A Mother's Prayer" by Nina Eckart is a prayer for the life of a son wounded in battle. Ellen Jakeman allows readers to feel a woman's relief when she finally hears from her absent loved one in "Your Letter." And "Let Us Have Peace" by Emily Hill Woodmansee is a plea to God as well as women to bring about a peaceful world. Peace to the soul is what Emmeline B. Wells in "Shadow-Land" and Augusta Joyce Crocheron in "Thoughts Within" pray for as both plead for insight and understanding. Meaning is clear in "Invocation, or the Eternal Father and Mother," Eliza R. Snow's profound meditation on godhood, immortality, and eternal relationships. The restored Church is central to Lu Dalton's "Woman," where she powerfully articulates women's subordinate position in the 1800s and asserts her belief that the gospel will ultimately recompense the injustices they have suffered. And in "The Relief Society," Ruth May Fox expresses gratitude for the organization that she believes elevates women's status and restores equality between women and men. Each poem resonates with modern readers, demonstrating the skill these women achieved as poets.

Like their nineteenth-century sisters, Mormon women of the twentieth century continued to claim poetry as their province. During the twentieth century, there were as many poems by women as by men published in Latter-day Saint venues for poetry, and Mormon women such as Carol Lynn Pearson and Emma Lou Thayne are among the most influential and well-known poets of the Latter-day Saints. In the 1985 Church hymnal, for example, there are twenty-two hymn texts written by men living when the hymnal was published and thirty hymn texts written by living women (the text of a hymn is a type of poem).

*Discoveries* includes a section of short biographical entries about each poet. An examination of the biographies shows how these women developed into serious and committed poets with significant achievements. Most showed an early interest in language and poetry and gained recognition for their poems in elementary or high school. It is significant that all the twentieth-century poets earned college degrees, including May Swenson, born in 1913, and Iris P. Corry, born in 1917. Some had teachers that influenced them, but others just began to read poetry. They read widely, benefiting both from the study of historical greats like Shakespeare, the King James Bible, Elizabeth Barrett Browning, and Gerard Manley Hopkins, and more modern and contemporary figures like Edna St. Vincent Millay, T. S. Eliot, Louise Glück, Mary Oliver, and Billy Collins. Thus, twentieth-century Mormon women poets have made themselves part of the larger tradition of contemporary American poetry.

It is a sign of the maturity and professionalism of these poets that publishing has been important to them. Many first saw their poems in high school or college literary magazines, then went on to publish in Mormon magazines and journals and finally in national literary journals. These twentieth-century poets have published over thirty collections of poetry, according to their biographical entries (which do not necessarily list all their published books). Of course, May Swenson's sixteen books are half of that total. May Swenson is the star of the group, her national reputation as a leading American poet demonstrated by her Guggenheim fellowship, Bolingen Prize, and MacArthur fellowship. In addition to Swenson, several other women have achieved national recognition for their poetry and prose, some have made a career of writing, and several have become professors or teachers. Many have chosen primarily to be homemakers and to make poetry an avocation. Whatever their life choices, all have demonstrated a love of and commitment to writing excellent poetry.

Which brings us to the later poetry. However different these poems are from each other, they all demonstrate a mastery of technique and craft in the presentation of subject. The rhyme, rhythms, and refrains of the formal poems seem to have been achieved without effort, so effective are they in presenting their language complexities. The two songs—"Song of Creation" by Linda Sillitoe and "Will you Remember" by Marilyn McMeen Brown—create lyrical patterns and repetitions that are a delight to follow. Penny Allen's blank verse poem "Blackberry" is dense and sophisticated in its depiction of Eve. May Swenson's "The Centaur" uses an occasional rhyme very subtly in the three-line stanzas as it re-creates Swenson's childhood play as both rider and horse, joining imagination and memory. Elouise Bell's "Psalm for a Saturday Night" and Virginia Maughan Kammeyer's "Morning Prayer" make use of the cadences of Biblical language to become true prayers. Susan Howe draws on scripture as well for her meditation on the creation, "Of the Beginning." The two sonnets—"A Lullaby in the New Year," also by Linda Sillitoe and "I Will One Day Be a Widow, Love," by Penny Allen—are fine examples of this difficult form. And the delicate rhymes in Karen Moloney's "Relinquishing" and the rhyme and repetition of Sally Taylor's villanelle "Fading Family Portrait" help the poets face and accept the death of beloved family members. The humorous poems in the collection are great fun, the light rhyming verse of Virginia Maughan Kammeyer and Jean Lauper presenting some of the ironic aspects of family life, and the two free verse poems— Mary Bradford's "Coming Apart Together" and Carol Lynn Pearson's "Mother's Post Pledge"—offering both humor and deeper insight.

The other free verse poems are similarly excellent, though in different ways. Emma Lou Thayne's "Sunday School Picture" is a long memoir of her childhood in Salt Lake City's Highland Park Ward. Marilyn Bushman-Carlton's "Summer School 1960" is also a memory of the time she realized as a teenager that some problems are not resolved happily. The spare language and imagery of Iris Parker Corry's "Nellie Unthank" fits this poem about the suffering and difficult life of this child of the Martin Handcart Company. In the opposite fashion, the rich imagery of Emma Lou Thayne's "To a Daughter About to Become a Missionary," of Meg Munk's poem sequence "One Year" (about her battle with cancer) and her catalogue of a mother's daily activities, "For Dad and Mother," and of Marilyn Bushman-Carlton's "Voluntary Poverty" and "Alisa Leaves for Medical School" makes these poems full portraits. Several of the poems work with extraordinary similes—Carol Clark Ottesen's "The Kiss" compares a first kiss to the flight of a flock of ducks, and the mother in Dawn Baker Brimley's "Not Far Behind" is like a minute hand of a clock, her daughter like the faster second hand. In four of the poems, the imagery takes on the echoes and additional meaning of symbols: in Elaine Christensen's "Newlyweds," the honeymooning couple are visited by a placid moose on their camping trip, a harbinger of their marital happiness; the stitches in Dixie Partridge's "Learning to Quilt" hold a family of many generations together; "The Shell in Silk" is Nancy Hanks Baird's metaphor for her mother's centrality and great value to her father; and in "Full Circle Summer," Dawn Baker Brimley's mother is evoked by a fruit tree so heavily laden with the fall crop that a part of it has broken.

But it is better to read these poems—and the nineteenth-century ones with which they are interwoven—than simply to read about them. We have titled this collection *Discoveries* because the poems are discoveries, in several senses of that word. Most of the nineteenth-century poems have been quite literally re-discovered, unearthed by the research of our historians. The twentieth-century poems, too, have been similarly re-discovered and brought together in this publication. In writing the poems, the poets themselves made illuminating discoveries as they looked at their subjects and articulated them in language. And finally, each of these poems will be, we hope, a discovery to the reader, through the art of poetry, of the complexities, joys, struggles, and spiritual power of Mormon women.

## Notes

1. See Maureen Ursenbach Beecher, "Poetry and the Private Lives: Newspaper Verse on the Mormon Frontier," *BYU Studies* 25 (Summer 1985): 55–65.

2. For overviews, see Susanna Morrill, "White Roses on the Floor of Heaven: Nature and Flower Imagery in Latter-day Saint Women's Literature, 1880–1920" (PhD diss., University of Chicago, Divinity School, 2002); and Julie Paige Hemming Savage, "'Yet I Must Submit': Mormon Women's Perspectives on Death and Dying, 1847–1900" (master's thesis, Brigham Young University, 1995). Projects on individual poets include Kylie Nielson Turley, "The Life and Literature of Josephine Spencer" (master's thesis, Brigham Young University, 1995); and Sheree Maxwell Bench, "'Woman Arise!': Political Work in the Writings of Lu Dalton" (master's thesis, Brigham Young University, 2002).

3. See Maureen Ursenbach Beecher, "Inadvertent Disclosure: Autobiography in the Poetry of Eliza R. Snow," *Dialogue* 23 (Spring 1990): 94–107; and Jill Mulvay Derr, "Form and Feeling in a Carefully Crafted Life: Eliza R. Snow's 'Poem of Poems,'" *Journal of Mormon History* 26 (Spring 2000): 1–39. The most thorough work on Snow is yet to come as Jill Mulvay Derr and Karen Lynn Davidson prepare a volume of nearly five hundred of her poems. This comprehensive anthology will provide historical, cultural, and theological context for Snow's work as well as literary analysis.

4. The *Contributor* (1854–1930) also published women's poetry.

5. Emmeline B. Wells, *Musings and Memories*, 2d ed. (Salt Lake

City: Deseret News, 1915), i; Augusta Joyce Crocheron, comp., *Representative Women of Deseret* (Salt Lake City: J. C. Graham, 1884), iii.

6. Crocheron, *Representative Women of Deseret,* iii; Miriam B. Murphy, "Sarah Elizabeth Carmichael: Poetic Genius of Pioneer Utah," in *Worth Their Salt: Notable but Often Unnoted Women of Utah,* ed. Colleen Whitley (Logan: Utah State University Press, 1996), 64.

7. Annie Wells Cannon, Preface, *Our Legacy: Relief Society Centennial Anthology of Verse by Latter-day Saint Women, 1835–1942* (Salt Lake City: General Board of Relief Society, 1941), vi.

# Acknowledgments

We thank the following organizations at Brigham Young University, which have also helped to sponsor this project:

- ❦ The College of Fine Arts
- ❦ The Department of Theatre, Film, and Media Arts
- ❦ The College of Humanities
- ❦ The Department of English
- ❦ The Women's Research Institute.

We are grateful for the support and guidance we received from Jill Mulvay Derr, Smith Institute Director; John W. Welch, Editor in Chief of BYU Studies; and Gideon Burton, Association for Mormon Letters president. We also express appreciation to Brad Westwood and the staff of L. Tom Perry Special Collections, Harold B. Lee Library, Brigham Young University.

# Beginning

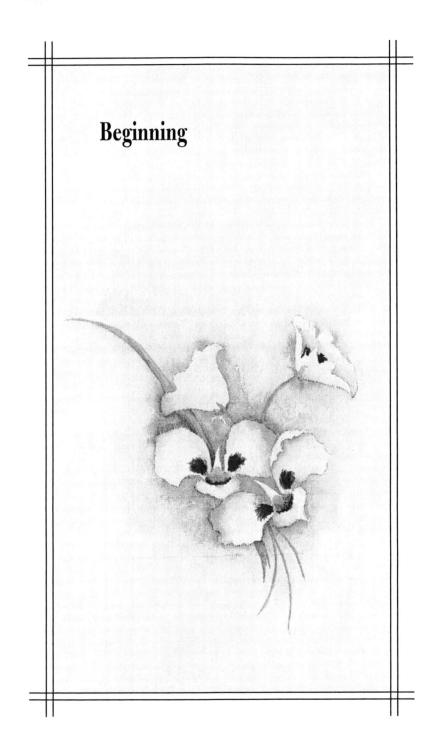

# Of the Beginning ❧

*Susan Elizabeth Howe*

O Daughters, I will speak
of excellent things. The opening
of my lips shall be from everlasting,
from the beginning or ever
the earth was.

When darkness was upon the face
of the void, we were there.
When there were no depths, we
exploded against the bleakness
of density.

We watched the gassy sweep
of the galaxy, loved the forming sun
for its light, the moon for its patience,
the stars for their distance
and immensity.

As Earth swirled in its sphere
we were centripetal. As seas
gathered together, we touched a finger
to the face of the deep. As clouds
meandered

into the sky, our cheeks moistened
in the mist. Bedrock settled
in our beds, and from us
soils learned to nourish.
We saw matter

organized—hills everlasting, fountains
of the deep. Matter inspirited
as flower, fish, bush, beast,
all bearing egg or seed.
These we gathered,

enfolding spheres of truth within
ourselves, prepared with wisdom,
the wisdom of God, the God of light,
the light of the daughter
and the dawn.

# Blackberry ℣

*Penny Allen*

Sucking darkness into swollen lobes,
It rides the cane over in its plumpness.
She wants it—enough to thread a careful hand
Through the thorns, etching a ragged red
Rivulet on the wrist and pricking tiny
Rubies where she wavers until her fingers
Lightly pluck it—thumb-pad pierced by a point
In the process. She pulls the berry back
Through close-woven briars; it stains startled
Fingers pinching at the pull of a thorny
Anchor. She plunks it into her wet mouth.
Delicious. More desirable than the first
Death she ate. Yet long after her tongue
Forgets the sweet, her throbbing thumb remembers
The pain, and still hungry, into the tangle
She flinches, sighing, "Oh, Eden, Eden."

# Woman

*Lu Dalton*

Woman is first to know sorrow and pain,
    Last to be paid for her labor,
First in self-sacrifice, last to obtain
    Justice, or even a favor.

First to greet lovingly man at his birth,
    Last to forsake him when dying,
First to make sunshine around his hearth,
    Last to lose heart and cease trying.

Last at the cross of her crucified Lord,
    First to behold him when risen,
First, to proclaim him to life restored,
    Bursting from death's gloomy prison.

First to seek knowledge, the God-like prize,
    Last to gain credit for knowing,
First to call children a gift from the skies,
    Last to enjoy their bestowing.

First to fall under the censure of God,
    Last to receive a full pardon,
First to kiss meekly the chastening rod,
    Thrust from her beautiful garden.

First to be sold for the wages of sin,
    Last to be sought and forgiven,
First in the scorn of her dear brother, man,
    Last in the kingdom of heaven.

So, a day cometh, a glorious day,
    Early perfection restoring—
Sin and its burdens shall be swept away,
    And love flow like rivers outpouring.

Then woman, who loves e'en thro' sorrow and shame,
    The crown of a queen will be wearing,
And love, freed from lust, a divinely pure flame,
    Shall save our sad earth from despairing.

That latter-day work is already begun,
    The good from the evil to sever,
The Word has gone forth that when all is done,
    The last shall be first, forever.

# Embryo

*Sally T. Taylor*

Creation.
Before it is, it moves.
Does it think as it
        turns its face?
Is its knee-jerk reflex?

What happens at these
        fibrillations?
Do teaspoon hands cup,
and fingers feel each
        its own movement?

It is still just before
the exodus, when the water
turns to blood.

    Firstborn,
the angel of death
stands ready before dawn.

# A Lullaby in the New Year ❧

*Linda Sillitoe*

One week is not too soon to learn a very
early language; for your spine to be aware
that a rocking chair means comfort and your wary
nerves want sleep. Nothing will disappear,
forsaking you to vast, fluorescent air
your fists and feet can't pummel. You shudder
at my kiss, a random bother in your hair.
I tell you this, my loud and little daughter,
you have now all there is: familiar dark,
a blanket's wings without, warm milk within,
balanced with your head in my hand's cup
in a second cradle of flesh and sound. We rock
and still you rage. I kiss your hair again.
All right, I whisper, accept, accept and sleep.

# When I Was a Child

# The Centaur 🦌

*May Swenson*

The summer that I was ten—
Can it be there was only one
summer that I was ten? It must

have been a long one then—
each day I'd go out to choose
a fresh horse from my stable

which was a willow grove
down by the old canal.
I'd go on my two bare feet.

But when, with my brother's jack-knife,
I had cut me a long limber horse
with a good thick knob for a head,

and peeled him slick and clean
except a few leaves for the tail,
and cinched my brother's belt

around his head for a rein,
I'd straddle and canter him fast
up the grass bank to the path,

trot along in the lovely dust
that talcumed over his hoofs,
hiding my toes, and turning

his feet to swift half-moons.
The willow knob with the strap
jouncing between my thighs

was the pommel and yet the poll
of my nickering pony's head.
My head and my neck were mine,

yet they were shaped like a horse.
My hair flopped to the side
like the mane of a horse in the wind.

My forelock swung in my eyes,
my neck arched and I snorted.
I shied and skittered and reared,

stopped and raised my knees,
pawed at the ground and quivered.
My teeth bared as we wheeled

and swished through the dust again.
I was the horse and the rider,
and the leather I slapped to his rump

spanked my own behind.
Doubled, my two hoofs beat
a gallop along the bank,

the wind twanged in my mane,
my mouth squared to the bit.
And yet I sat on my steed

quiet, negligent riding,
my toes standing the stirrups,
my thighs hugging his ribs.

At a walk we drew up to the porch.
I tethered him to a paling.
Dismounting, I smoothed my skirt

and entered the dusky hall.
My feet on the clean linoleum
left ghostly toes in the hall.

*Where have you been?* said my mother.
*Been riding,* I said from the sink,
and filled me a glass of water.

*What's that in your pocket?* she said.
*Just my knife.* It weighted my pocket
and stretched my dress awry.

*Go tie back your hair,* said my mother,
and *Why is your mouth all green?*
*Rob Roy, he pulled some clover
as we crossed the field,* I told her.

# Sunday School Picture

*Emma Lou Thayne*

1               Our Ward housed
the biggest Sunday School the Church has ever
let exist, and one Sunday morning a thousand
of us hipped into the breathless benches
and undulated into the foyer, anteroom,
recreation hall, and up onto the indignant stage
a thousand Mormon heads away from the pulpit.

                     In the picture
that President Heber J. Grant had them take
that auspicious day (three shots overlapping)
I came out twice, being on the edge of two of them,
and Mother always said that would guarantee me
two chances at perfection, but I being seven
at the time figured so? and went on becoming
two people instead.

2               One of me would chin
my fretted flimsiness the forty-three times
my brothers said I should be able to
on the banister in the empty entry of the Ward,
and blithely loosen the screen from inside
the classroom while my Primary teacher
was rasping at Donnie Rohlfing,

so my brothers
and I and certain franchised friends could
scrunch in later and titter nonsense from
the palsied pulpit and play The Happy Farmer
with our pleated fingers on the cool black pedals
of the organ, and with rapid eyes see what other
kinds of bathrooms looked like, and run tautly for our
window if Mr. Tomlinson came clinking in,
and then try not to sit by Richard when I needed
to be nice in church

because he was the brother
that I got the giggles with like when we sang
You-hoo unto Jesus and had to leave all the time
hunching up the searing aisle acting like
we had the nosebleed, and Richard who was five
in First Grade when I was four in Kindergarten
smiled the teacher into promoting me into
his class (no one seemed to mind as long as I
could read the flash cards)

so I could be
on first and catch the siren balls he practiced
on me in our shivering front room where no one ever
threw anything except when Father thought
the quickest way to get me dressed for church
was to juggle my patented leather paraphernalia
at me saying Think fast!

so I'd snatch them on
before they dropped to prove I could, and then
race across the mud-hard fields to beat the organ's
going silent whispering its Sunday sentence.

3              The other me sedately
bathed my Di Dee Doll till her left eye
washed away, and played house with Corinne
at least seventeen hours a week in the tolerant
trailer her father built, and hated it when Marilyn
Mason (it must have been because of her wet palms
that stuck to things) beat me once a day
all summer at jacks,

        and lady-like
read Polly Anna, certain of a tunnel (probably
under our hollyhocks) and wrote a poem
drying my tortuous ringlets by the radiator
in the bathroom about spilling batter
on the blue kitchen floor that pale Miss Crawford
announced I must have copied somewhere,

and that me sat in buttoned velvet memorizing
the swollen arch of the ward chapel that cupped
the painting of the Sacred Grove where green
bumped into blue like my 500 piece puzzle with 200
desperate pieces of sky,

and hoped that
the deacons were noticing that I could read
the words to I Know That My Redeemer Lives,
which I wondered why we sang all four verses to
even though I was sure I guess I did know,
and recited a two-and-a-half minute ordeal
that my mother knew I knew on Why I Want
To Be Baptized,

which I didn't because of
the hospital and Richard who was in there
and couldn't be baptized with me, and pushed
one fidget finger at a time into the tempting
screw holes in the boring bench in front,
and dangled and waved absently with the other
eight-and-unders in the choir seats at our
determinedly non-noticing mothers,

and that me
made handkerchief dolls with my eyes closed
during the prayer and searched the sacrament
for the bread without a crust and held the rim
of the kiss-size cup against my lip and swallowed
slow to let it trickle down and feel like what
they said it should, and tried to think of Jesus
all white like in the Grove, not with his beard
crumpled on his collar bone, dead.

4           Sometimes I look
at that thousand-peopled picture when I'm sorting
things and marvel a lot, and even otherwise, I find
myself saying, Highland Park Ward, my roller skates
still rattle down your dented driveway, and
my absent waiting is sometimes done against
the brown banisters below the Garden of Gethsemane
in your raised entry,

           and mostly, your organ
churns under its outside loft across the filled
fields where our short-cuts are long buried
in old foundations,

           and like the green-grained oak
of your chapel doors, it closes with gentle right
my separateness and gathers my wandering
double selves together.

# On My Fourteenth Birthday ❦

*Lula Greene Richards*

My hand with a bouquet of flowers,
    My heart with a sunbeam's bright ray;
Thus innocent, happy, and careless,
    My childhood is passing away.

Ah! friends, gentle friends, I am noting,
    How time doth not pause or delay;
But each is a mark for his changes,
    My childhood is passing away.

May I ponder with wiser reflections,
    Yet with heart just as innocent say,
When gazing at time in the future,
    Bright youth, thou art passing away.

And when this earth-life shall be ending,
    Like th' close of a long summer's day,
Stepping from time to eternity,
    Just on the brink may I say,

While my hands clasp flowers immortal,
    Truth's flowers, which cannot decay,
And my heart basks in faith's golden glory,
    Life, death, ye are passing away.

# Reaching

# Woman's Sphere ❧

*Lu Dalton*

Tell me what is woman's sphere?
What path was she designed to tread?
What may she hope? What must she fear?
What may she do and what must dare
To win her daily dole of bread?

. . . . . . . . . . . . . . . . . . . . . . . . . . . . . . . . .

Is she but fit to sweep and sew,
To spread her master's table well,
To go and come, to come and go,
On one unvaried round, and grow
In nothing good if nothing ill?

Has she no mind to cultivate?
No heart for fatherland to glow?
No int'rest in the future fate
Of sons and daughters, that her state
Is almost slavery, vile and low?

. . . . . . . . . . . . . . . . . . . . . . . . . . . . . . . . .

As plants untended droop and fade,
And weeds choke out most precious seed,
So woman's mind, a desert made
By long suppression, needs the aid
Of cultivation broad and deep.

. . . . . . . . . . . . . . . . . . . . . . . . . . . . . . . . .

Let woman's sphere, then, not be small;
Her powers developed, not confined,
Her intellect, will, body, all
Emancipated from the thrall
Which far too long has round them twined.

Whatever she can well perform,
Whatever she aspires to do,
Whate'er expands, protects from harm
Or gives her life an ample form
Is well, O man, thrice well for you.

When your mind's culture is complete,
Your nature polished and refined,
For mate in life 'tis surely meet
You have a soul, not simply sweet,
But strong and noble, heart and mind.

No shadow, charming toy nor slave
Can ever be companion true;
To fit her for her duties grave,
More light and room must woman have—
To walk side by side with you.

. . . . . . . . . . . . . . . . . . . . . . . . . . . . . . . . . .

# An Apology

*Lula Greene Richards*

Did I stay too long in the school room
    After the lessons were through,
Leaving my mother and sisters
    With all the work to do?
And has it vexed you, mother,
    My mother, so patient and true?

Forgive me, my mother and sisters,
    Smile kindly and gently speak;
I'll try to do better tomorrow
    And all the rest of the week,
If my wayward mind and feelings
    Do not play me another freak.

The children were hard to manage,
    Heedless and dull today;
It seemed they could think of nothing
    Except their love for play,
Out doors the birds and flowers
    And sunshine were all so gay.

And after the lessons were ended
  They sought of youth's charms the chief,
While to rest in the quiet school room
  Was to me a blessed relief,
And the time slipped by unnoticed,
  The moments appeared so brief.

And I have been writing something
  Which will likely enough be read
By our children's children
  After we all are dead;
And must I think I should have been
  Washing dishes instead?

# The Bachelor Maid ❧

*Ruth May Fox*

Here is a song to the bachelor maid
　　The maiden neat and prim;
Who treads the earth with modest air,
　　Deigns not to look at *him*.

She will not wed when love is not
　　But struggles through the strife
Alone, and who so lone as she
　　Who's never called a wife?

And who so wise as the bachelor maid,
　　Or who so truly brave?
She holds the world or stirs it up
　　With sayings terse and grave.

She leads reforms for woman-kind,
　　She mothers all the race;
She trains young ideas how to shoot
　　And keeps them going apace.

And many a father holds her hand,
　　Many a path is smoothed;
And many a mother's downward years
　　By a bachelor maid are soothed.

So here's a song to the bachelor maid,
　　She's honest to the core;
She finds her place in the world's work
　　And asks for nothing more.

# Will you Remember? ❧

*Marilyn McMeen Brown*

Will you remember, lovely love?
Before your kingdom come?
If you remember not one day
I remember one.

The sun and stars together
Beneath the deafening sky
Poured night and day and weather
Into a lovely cry.

And wild asparagus, rhubarb
Became our only meal.
We sat beneath the wattles
You built upon the hill.

You touched my hand and loved me.
I answered with a kiss.
You said, "I'm yours forever."
Do you remember this?

The rhubarb long has rotted,
The wattles tumbled through.
And so our love has died its death
And found its graveyard too.

We buried it in summer
Beneath the maple tree
About our shade and underneath
A short eternity.

# April Flowers ❧

*Sarah Carmichael*

Pale flowers, pale flowers, ye came too soon;
    The North, with icy breath,
Hath whispered hoarsely through the skies
    A word that spoke of death.
Ye came too soon—the Spring's first glance,
    In this cold clime of ours,
Is but the sheen of Winter's lance—
    Ye came too soon, pale flowers!

. . . . . . . . . . . . . . . . . . . . . . . . . . . . . . . . . .

Pale, blighted flowers, the summer time
    Will smile on brighter leaves;
They will not wither in their prime,
    Like a young heart that grieves;
But the impulsive buds that dare
    The chill of April showers,
Breathe woman-love's low martyr prayer—
    I kiss your leaves, pale flowers.

# Summer School, 1960 ❧

*Marilyn Bushman-Carlton*

Supper watermelon pink on the tongue,
I meet Linda at Julian's Drug.
Caressing bottles of Orange Crush
we mosey to Vet's Field
where lights flood the boys' softball game.
Yet to come are my first airplane ride,
my friend, Terry's, death in Vietnam,
Aunt Beverly's double mastectomy.

Beneath a sycamore we sit,
almond arms bared, jeans rolled thin
above the knees. Whispered news
*Suzanne's parents getting a divorce*
falls like a third strike.

We click off all the answers:
>            *Don't get fat*
>            *Or sit apart in the car like old-marrieds*
>            *Never curlers or cold cream to bed*
>            *Don't be too tired or have a headache*

I take the long way home. Mrs. Smuin's
chartreuse roses hammer my head,
children's nine o'clock faces are dirtied,
mud oozes between their toes.
Over and over I try to twist
the melancholy mood of cricket chirr,
I want them to lighten up, to sing
*It isn't so    It isn't so*

## Cactus Blossoms.

Poets have sung with tuneful lay
Of the lily fair, of the rose's spray ;
But I my humble off'ring bring
To the lovely shrine of the Desert Queen.

'Mong bare red rocks of the barren hill,
'Mid desert sands so lone and still,
Where the rabbit, wolf, and lizard roam,
Thou delightest most to make thy home.

Queen art thou of a regal line,
In thy robes of satin so soft and fine ;
Set on a throne of emerald green,
And guarded thine armed hosts between.

Writ on thy throne, our common lot,
Thy mandate, " Beware that ye touch me not,
Or the lesson learn, 'tis a thorny lane
He needs must tread who the prize would gain."

In the dreary prospect of greys and browns,
Thou art like a smile amid angry frowns ;
The gleam of hope that forbids despair,
Or a dream of love in our world of care.

—Julia A. Macdonald.

Source: *Songs and Flowers of the Wasatch*, ed. Emmeline B. Wells (Salt Lake City: George Q. Cannon, 1893), 15.

# First Bliss

# First Date ❧

*Virginia Maughan Kammeyer*

How can I go to the Gold and Green Ball
With the son of a friend of my *mother?*
He'll either be early, or not come at all,
Or else he'll be late—Oh, brother!

Is this why I worried and struggled to grow up,
And practiced my charm routine for?
To wait for a date with a guy who won't show up—
Is *this* what I turned sixteen for?

What if his hands are clammy and sticky?
What if he turns out to really be icky?
I'm having a blind date with *somebody's son!*
I'd rather go out with Attila the Hun!

Oh, all right, I'll *go*—but it sure doesn't strike me.
The doorbell! Oh, Mom! Do you think that he'll like me?

# The Kiss ❦

*Carol Clark Ottesen*

We brush like velvet cattails

in the wind

and rise like restless mallards

on the marsh,

first one, then two

until

five hundred fluttering wings

in one immense polyphony of sound

block out the world

then

settle

like a feather on a leaf,

quaking and quivering

with joy.

# Betrothed 🌿

*Augusta Joyce Crocheron*

Why is it, that through all the day
    And waking hours of night,
My thoughts run all the same sweet way,
    One path of calm delight?
A few short months ago, and we
    As strangers met and passed,
No thrill of joy awoke in me,
    No thought on me you cast.

But strangely, fate has caught and tied
    Together our life threads
In a sweet love knot, nor denied
    Friends' blessings on our heads.
Strangers a year ago, to-day
    I sit and slow recall
Our walk beneath the starry way
    And words your lips let fall.

Yet stay, my pencil! there may lean
    Some spirit reading this,
Whose envious power might intervene
    To part my life from his.
No further be the secret read,
    Until himself shall lay
His crown of love upon my head,
    To bless my life alway.

# Newlyweds

*Elaine Wright Christensen*

From Tony Grove we hiked two miles
into White Pine Lake,
buried, deep green, behind Mt. Gog
and its twin peak Mt. Magog.
We pitched our two-man tent
near the water
and built a fire of hot coals
for tinfoil dinners.

At dusk a moose came crashing
through the undergrowth,
waded out into the dark water
to feed on moss dripping
like long mermaid hair
from his rounded wet muzzle.
He heard us. Looked our way.
Stopped chewing
and, unconcerned, lowered his head.
We watched him feed,
nuzzling in the shallows,
till his form lost shape in darkness.
Out of the night
we heard him splash,
step by step, up the stream bed
that fed the lake now gone to glass.

It was an omen, a blessing,
that we would know joy.
And the stars knew.
They turned themselves on
for us,
while we watched,
one by one.

# A Child of My Body

# The Baby

*Augusta Joyce Crocheron*

O, what is all this noise about?
    The house is full of joy to-day;
I hear the laugh and call ring out—
    They cannot hear a word I say.
I cannot read, or think, or write,
    In all this racket full of fun;
I really wish that it were night,
    And they were sleepy, every one.

I don't know what I want to do,
    For hard as I may try to think,
The sound of those boot heels goes through
    My ears so sharp, it makes me wink!
And I know just how the hair I curled
    So silken smooth an hour ago,
For a rosy-cheeked, dear little girl,
    Is tossing, flying, high and low.

And baby's as wild as either one,
    The darling little household prince!
O'er racket of chairs that fall as they run,
    He shrieks with joy; I fairly wince.
Why! "The baby is walking alone to-day,"
    The first time in his little life;
Ah! the thought near takes my breath away,
    And the happy words cut like a knife.

"O! aint you proud ma'am?" Susan asks,
    "And how surprised his pa will be!"
And she forgets her crowding tasks,
    And gives him kisses two and three.
Proud? when his first steps alone
    Open my eyes to the truth, heart-sore:
He out of his babyhood has grown,
    And needs my leading hand no more.

And it seems as though the baby boy,
    I have loved so silently and well,
Must have been a dream-child, and the joy,
    The year has passed an unbroken spell.
And now, instead of a babe in my arms,
    Starting in sleep when I lay him down,
My heart is thrilled with swift alarms,
    While steady and sure, he runs around.

O my baby! to think that you,
    Would choose to slide from your mother's knee;
Would rather shout with those tomboys, two,
    Than here in her loving arms to be.
When did you change, you butterfly,
    From a cradled thing to a thing of flight?
No, no, I cannot laugh while I
    Look on the new and doubtful sight.

The wide earth luring thee to go;
    Temptation's smile; ambition's call;
And thou a man! life's ways must know,
    Must meet its lessons one and all.
And I have been thy highest love!
    How weak, alas! thy mother's arms,
They cannot keep thee. Lord above,
    Lead Thou my darling safe from harm.

# For Dad and Mother 🦥

*Margaret Rampton Munk*

Weary at evening,
After the alarm clock,
Oatmeal,
Lunch pails,
Car pool,
Grocery bags
Up ten steps
Two by two,
Tuna fish
And noodle soup,
School bus,
Socks and blue jeans,
Swimming lesson,
"Papa Haydn"
At the keyboard,
Stacatto oratory
From the first grade reader,
Knights in armor
On their sofa cushion steeds,
Urgent calls
From six-year-old admirers,
Skinned knees

And Band-Aids,
Broken bike chains,
Missing mittens,
Quarrels of unknown origin,
Kitchen strewn with leavings
Of creative genius,
Frying pan
And soapsuds,
Fork on the left,
Spoon on the right,
Gymnastics after dinner,
Toothpaste and pajamas,
Stories,
Singing,
And the very latest tactics
For bedtime delay—

I do well to remember:

Someone thought
That I was worth it,
Every day.

# What Are the Fathers About?

*Emily Hill Woodmansee*

The manifold duties of mothers
Are re-echoed from pulpit to stand
One wonders, who hears it so often,
If no Fathers are left in the land
We're thankful of course for good counsel
Suggestions are good in their place
But if woman is only a helpmeet
Oh, why should she shoulder the race

One would think that the care of their children
Was a tax altogether too small
To claim from the Lords of Creation
Any time or attention at all
Our requisite patience and duty
We hear both within and without
While mothers must needs be perfection
Pray, what are the Fathers about

Tis refreshing to read in the Bible
How Solomon, Royal as wise,
Instructed his offspring and left them
The proverbs that ages shall prize
He settled not down to the notion
That to others His duty belonged
That because of a mother's devotion
With cares she must ever be thronged

Or, he might have been loth to consider
That women were capable—quite
Of bearing and teaching his children
Whatever was needful and right
Perchance we should even be grateful
That we live in these civilized times
When society claims of the Mother
An account for all juvenile crimes

Were men building kingdoms and empires
Or creating new planets for space
We'd do both as father and mother
Double duty, and deem it our place
But patience, herself, grows tired of suggestions
Grows weary though nought is their price
Tis the fruit of our sober reflections
That *help* is ahead of advice.

There are Fathers we know who are faithful
Be sure, we don't mean them at all
This cap wasn't fashioned to fit them
And for many we trust tis too small
But that Sires owe their children attention
Twould be folly to question or doubt
And *some* might enquire of their conscience
Oh what are we fathers about.

# Not Far Behind

*Dawn Baker Brimley*

Now that you are seventeen,
an important age,
you sweep by me
in your hurry to get places.
Sometimes I would like to follow,
but your world is yours
alone.

I think of you as a second hand
on a clock.
And I am the minute hand,
not too far behind,
glad for the moments
when we make brief contact,
yet knowing your revolutions
will always out-distance me.

You are an extension of me,
(though the psychiatrists
say that should never be)
and sometimes I feel you
as though you were my arm.
Especially when you are hurt
my senses are alive.
Then you are like
an ache in my arm
which I would heal
if I could.

In your haste, please remember
I am here, not too far behind you.
When you feel you want us to make contact,
tell me so,
and I will run,
breaking all the laws of nature.
Like a minute hand gone wild
I will run
to catch up with you.

## Voluntary Poverty ❧

*Marilyn Bushman-Carlton*

Justin steps into January
with would-be icicles dripping
from the tips of his hair,
a backward cap covering his soggy crown.
Sixteen, he is trying to master
the poverty look he sees on the news.
Homelessness beckons—
a brave, romantic adventure.
The chores of finding daily food and a roof—
wilderness experiences in the city.
Disease is a short rest from classes
and from his job sweeping floors after school.
*Have a good day,* I say
and watch as he walks away,
the crotch of his X-tra Large pants swinging
between the clothespins of his knees,
the waist nearly a foot south
and cinched like a knapsack.

# To My Dear Children ❧

*Virginia Maughan Kammeyer*

I used to miss my freedom
As I hauled you near and far;
But, suddenly, you're teenagers,
And now I miss the car.

# The Debt ❧

*Jean Gordon Lauper*

Daughters Dear, when you were young
    How hard for you I worked.
I bathed and cooked and washed and scrubbed
    And not a task I shirked.

I always thought, "When they grow up
    Oh how they'll work for me.
Then I'll not be the household drudge,
    Rough hands and calloused knee"

Now you are grown—You precious things
    And is the debt repaid?
Not yet—but girls it's GONNA be,
    Dad's hiring me a MAID.

# Devotional

# Morning Prayer ❧

*Virginia Maughan Kammeyer*

Dear Lord,
Who took the moon and stars
And put them in their place;
Whose ruling law is Order
Through infinities of space;
The monumental daily tasks
Help me to face, I pray,
And strive to push the chaos back
As dawn bursts forth each day.

# Psalm for a Saturday Night

*Elouise Bell*

Bring forth thy Sabbath, O Lord,
    For I am ready.

I have anointed my head with jubilation
    Pressed from thy ripest blessings.
My soul has been washed in thy raining grace,
    And I am clean and shining.
O deliver thy Sabbath, for I await!

I have clothed me in a garment of repentance;
    The ragged sins of this week have I cast off.
My hair is perfumed with the unguent of forgiving:
    There remains no burr or tangle to snarl the sweep of love.
O sanctify thy Sabbath, and let its mantle fall about me!

I have adorned my hand with jewels of compassion.
    My feet are shod with eagerness for thy service.
Here in the pulsing darkness I bate my breath
    And urge the stars on in their passage.

Bring forth thy Day, O Lord,
    For thy servant waits.

# The Relief Society 🌿

*Ruth May Fox*

Author of Justice, God of Liberty,
In gratitude Thy daughters bend the knee,
That Thou hast cleft the galling servile chain,
And lifted woman to her place again.

Thy righteous word doth narrowness efface,
Man's equal she; the mother of the race
Could be no less, since sage and seer agree,
That what she is mankind will surely be.

Man's not without the woman in the Lord;
Nor was the Church in Latter-days restor'd
Complete, until the prophet "turned the key",
Which ope'd the door for sex equality;
And organized our saintly Sisterhood
A helpmeet to the priestly Brotherhood;
Each in its sphere to forward God's great cause
Until the world should recognize His laws.

. . . . . . . . . . . . . . . . . . . . . . . . . . . . . . . . . .

For this Society which Thou didst frame
And make a pillar in Thy Church, Thy name,
Dear Lord, we glorify; and humbly bow
That thus, Thou placed Thy seal on woman's brow
And clothed her in the robes of charity
Pronounced her Thine, a child of Deity.

# Release

# Mother's Post Pledge ❦

*Carol Lynn Pearson*

Look
I hereby:

Cross out my critique
    of your performance
Toss out my agenda
    for your life
Tear up my list of
    things you need to do
Swear up and down
    I will not do it again.

Of course it's odd
But for a while there
I mistook myself for God.

# To a Daughter about to Become a Missionary  
*for Dinny*

*Emma Lou Thayne*

Twenty-two, she sleeps upstairs
between the windows of my life,
in the sleigh bed that has housed
the comings of four generations

like exotic potted plants chosen
to color bedrooms with blossoming.
Two high birdseye dressers contain her,
drawers closed on pink turtle-necks

and speedos, walls of rackets and mustachioed
smiles. Mirrors swing her reflection
of medicated soap and squashed rollers
dropping away from night to issue

a daytime Pietà laughing and grieving,
beautifully turned out, surprising as
a crocus in snow. Other rights postponed,
the child that God intended will wear

the sanctity of the blue blazer,
skirted and frocked, innocent in her
expectation. Of course we have known
she would leave, the covers

opened and closed. It is time.
The horizon whitens. Water runs.
This is morning. She will see. France
will tell. She is changing to

the garments of The Word, will take on
the terrors of the verb To Be,
not knowing yet why departure
spells return. Five-hundred forty-seven

and a half days. She will open wide
her arms sweatered for the long cold.
The darkness will lighten and she will become
the waiting room for the willing stranger.

Kisses blow like blizzards through my empty
spaces saying God, please. I go up to sit on
her suitcase that will not close,
press messages into her shoes,

the smell of kitchen under the leather
of her scriptures. Snow has made feathers
of trees. She lifts the sleepy shadow
of her face, steps into the air. She is gone.

I do not dare breathe in the bedroom.
Or move. Only to listen to the runners
of the sleigh bed following her.

And me unable to make it for fear
of blanketing the sweet shiny smell
of Dr. Pepper lip gloss beneath the down,
above the furrows of knees along the floor.

# Alisa Leaves for Medical School

*Marilyn Bushman-Carlton*

What would Grandmother think,
my sending a daughter off
the way she sent hers to Salt Lake
with only a battered trunk
and what she'd learned from a small town?
What would she say, a daughter flying
over the puzzle of states
she, too, studied in school,
their women's lives lost
in histories logged by men?
What advice would Mother give?

My daughter leaves, not tucked
in the rib of a husband's hopes,
but chasing her own,
less-accustomed dream.

I rearrange the furniture,
shift the bed near a sunny window,
re-pot the schefflera.

Grandmother and Mother must have done this, too,
not so much to utilize the empty space,
but more to camouflage it—
the way the picky eater moves unwanted food
around her big white plate,
shifting this and that

to fool the eye.

# A Mother's Farewell

*Emily Hill Woodmansee*

*Mary Blakemore to her daughter Mary Ann,
on the occasion of her marriage and leaving
the home of her childhood*

I cannot, cannot see thee go,
    My cherished darling child;
I cannot, cannot say farewell
    In accents calm and mild.

My heart is torn with such distress
    As mothers only feel,
Who see their loved ones shelterless,
    Exposed to every ill.

How gladly would I shelter thee
    From every grief and care!
But now thy home far hence will be
    Alas, I know not where.

But this I know, my aching heart
    Thine absence will bemoan;
The very sunshine will depart
    With thee, my loved, my own.

Yet, 'tis not for myself I grieve
    Forbid the selfish thought;
Nay, 'tis for thee, continually,
    My soul with pain is fraught.

To sorrow, oft there is an end,
    To trouble, some relief;
But well, my child, you comprehend,
    Mine is no common grief.

By day and night my thoughts will rise;
    My very breath shall be
A prayer to God, the good and wise,
    To guide thy destiny.

God grant the lessons learned from me,
    E'en from thy earliest youth,
May yet repeat themselves to thee,
    As words of light and truth.

In God's own way, in God's own time
    Oh, may I yet behold
My darling child, my rescued lamb,
    Safe in the Savior's fold.

Be sure of this, where e'er you roam,
    Or whatsoe'er your lot:
There still will be a place for thee
    Within your mother's cot.

Oh! think it not a little thing,
    Thus from a child to part;
You cannot tell, how deep Love's well
    Within a mother's heart.

# The Mother Pioneers.

Ah have you ever heard in song or story
The names of those, our Mother Pioneers,
Who left their homes to share in unknown sorrows
Of hunger, weariness, and trembling fears?
Each shared the toil, drank the same cup of sorrow.

Their hands were white, but not too white to toil,
Their garments coarse, but made them seem more fair,
Their voices clear, lifted in songs of praise,
Thrilled into rapture all the desert air;
And their reward was love's untarnished flame,
And in their souls the peace of those who've trod
With all Christ's armor on, day after day,
Unshodden through the Holy House of God.

—Ellen Jakeman.

Source: *Songs and Flowers of the Wasatch,* ed. Emmeline B. Wells (Salt Lake City: George Q. Cannon, 1893), 25.

# Bowed Down with Sorrow

# Thoughts Within

*Augusta Joyce Crocheron*

As some poor laborer's sightless babe
Wakes from its pallet on the floor
In fear, to find itself alone,
And gropes the open door to find;
Reaching anon the empty air
To clutch; seeking something to grasp
To aid it in its search; and then,
Wearying in its efforts vain,
It lifts its plaintive, grieving wail;
Then pauses, listening softly for
Its mother's answering voice; so I
Kneel down before Thine unseen throne—
So I call to Thee in my prayer
Earnest and deep, yet humble too;
And listen with that inner ear
Far in the soul's remotest depth.
Not for Thy voice to sweep to earth
Answering to my human cry,
As angels in the old times did,
When men were truly, purely Thine;
But for an influence, sweet and still,
To lead my groping soul aright.

As though I, clinging to some hand,
Across a torrent spanned but by
A slender tree's decaying trunk,
Looking not to the shore beyond,
Nor turning, though the pine tree shriek
And wave her arms, and writhe in the grasp
Of the dark storm-fiend, strong in his wrath—
Nor on the current swift beneath,
Lest I should, swooning, fall and sink;
But only where my steps should be.
So will I, clinging, follow Thee
Across life's deep, unmindful of
The strife below.

# Shadow-Land ❧

*Emmeline B. Wells*

. . . . . . . . . . . . . . . . . . . . . . . . . . . . . . . . . .

Oh, what is this longing, this yearning to know?
    This germ of an impulse we cannot restrain?
And why should it haunt me and follow me so,
    If the quest it awakens is fruitless and vain?
Nay, I feel that beyond the scope of my dreaming,
The star of intelligence onward is streaming.

I call in the night-time for strength from on high,
    To open the flood-gates of knowledge for me.
I wait, and I listen, but only the sigh
    Of the murmuring winds, in quaint melody,
Chants the song of my heart, tho' its music is clear,
We've lived heretofore in some loftier sphere.

. . . . . . . . . . . . . . . . . . . . . . . . . . . . . . . . . .

# Nellie Unthank ✹

### Iris P. Corry

aged ten,
walked, starved, froze
with the Martin Company
and left her parents in shallow graves
near the Sweetwater.

The Richards on First South
hugged their children's heads to muffle
Nellie, strapped to a board, without anesthetic,
screaming, her frost-black feet
removed with a butcher knife
and a carpenter's saw.

After that she walked on her knees,

married in polygamy to
William Unthank (of Cedar City)
who took her home to one room with a dirt floor.
She damped and scraped that floor
hard and smooth as sandstone,
washed it every day;
clean muslin curtains at the window,
on goods box cupboards.

Saturday nights the hearth whitened
and Nellie made her way
knitting, crocheting, carding wool,
kneeling by the washtub set on blocks
scrubbing townspeople's clothes on the board
and trading a yeast start for
a handful of sugar sent in the jar.

Said *never* to another operation—
waddled on leather kneepads in her little skirt
dragging her unhealed stumps
or pushed herself on a board on wheels.

Once a year Nellie and her six children cleaned
the meeting house.
The boys fetched water;
Annie, Martha, Polly washed the windows.
Nellie scrubbed the floor.

# Learning to Quilt ❧

*Dixie L. Partridge*

> *Times goes one way only, but we*
> *go two: . . . we drowse in care of our dreams—*
> *their sheltering flamboyant wings*
> *stretched over us, one in the past*
> *and one in the future.*
> —William Matthews

The patchwork, stretched on frames,
crowds furniture and all essential work
to edges; farmhouse windows in old lace
cast filigree on pastels of *nine-patch-stars.*
"You need a thimble," says my mother,
pleased to pass on the tiny stitches
that hold a quilt for generations.

Pattern names are italic in my memory:
*the rambler, jacob's ladder, flock-of-geese,*
but I can't place them with their quilts—
my grandmothers gone, Aunt Lena 82,
Mary in her final bed with cancer.
I imagine them wrapped in quilts
in their graves, carrying the permanence
of fingers ever stitching,
ever certain.

Nights, we are hemmed to dreams
overlaid with the calico and flannel
of distant relatives; appliques
from christening gowns, the old wools
of the fathers' first suits.

# A Mother's Prayer 🌱

*Nina Eckart*


Oh! March winds blow, blow strong I pray,
And waft a message far away
To distant lands, where now there lay
A soldier, sick and wounded—
Oh! fan his fevered brow and give
Him strength to rally and to live.

Oh! March winds blow and softly sigh,
And tell him that he must not die.
Oh! tell him if he'll only try,
That God may let him rally.
Tell him of the love that waits
To greet him at his dear home gate.

March winds sing to him a song,
And tell him of a love so strong,
A love which waiting, yearning longs
For his return.
And should he hear the death knell sound,
Oh! sing and make his heart rebound.

But wind, oh! take for me a prayer
To One above, oh! bear, please bear
Just once for me a message there
Unto the King,
Oh! tell Him all my life I give,
If He will let my loved one live.

# Your Letter

*Ellen Jakeman*

Alone in my room when the day was done,
    Free from the glances of critical eyes,
My armor of strength and my shield of pride
Were broken and scattered on every side.
    And pity and mercy seemed fled the skies,
The face you have kissed was drenched with tears,
    The form you have pressed was cold with despair.
    Life seemed gloomy and death seemed fair.
Too pitiless were the advancing years
Trooping out of the future, calling my name,
Beloved of my soul, when your letter came.

Ere the seal was broken, I knew whose hand
    Had written the lines that my eyes should see
Whose heart and soul in the hour of pain,
    In electric currents flowed out to me,
Back to my heart's red core, the blood
Rushed in an eager tumultuous flood;
    I spoke to you, kissed you, embraced you again
And read by numberless tokens and signs
The message, unwritten, between the lines.
    And gnawing anguish that has no name
    Died suddenly when your letter came.

I stood in your presence and felt no need
    Of my armor of strength or my shield of pride,
Your faith was my armor, your love was my shield,
    Hope's brilliant star was my trusted guide.
We may climb the hill by diverging paths,
    The hill of life to its loftiest tower;
But I never will know pain more complete
I never will know a bliss more sweet,
    Than was crowded into that one short hour
Till I slept, and my eyelids were gently pressed
By the dream-angel's rosy fingers blessed;
    My last thought, dear, was your whispered name,
    And peace was mine, when your letter came.

# Let Us Have Peace 🪶

*Emily Hill Woodmansee*

*"Blessed are the peacemakers, for they
shall be called the children of God."*
                                        —Jesus

. . . . . . . . . . . . . . . . . . . . . . . . . . . . . . . .

  "Let us have peace."
      Can heaven reject the prayer?
Can heaven ignore the widow's piteous moan?
Or disregard the orphan's grievous cry?
God sees His children's suffering everywhere,
The mournful sigh ascends to heaven's white throne.
God's plans are surely broader than our own;
      Can aught His love outvie?

  "Let us have peace."
      Let men their wrath restrain,
Let the world's sisterhood their efforts blend.
That strife may wane and happiness increase.
Ambitious greed, that would advantage gain
Must loose its hold, ere direful war will end;
Inspire the race, Almighty Lord and Friend!
      To speed the reign of peace.

# The Spirit of Sleep.

WHO is it that comes in shadowy robes,
  With a spell silent and deep,
Wrapping our forms in a mystic trance?
  'Tis the mighty spirit of sleep.

He seals the eyes that are wet with tears,
  And those where gladness beams,
And by a wave of his scepter-wand
  We soar to the land of dreams.

'Tis then the weary mourner finds,
  A brief respite from care;
And dreams perchance of a voice beloved,
  Or a face that was sweet and fair.

The sultan may lie on his downy bed
  With curtains of tinted glow,
The beggar may rest her weary bones,
  'Neath a coverlet of snow.

But potent the nectar his chalice holds,
  Solace to all he brings,
And visits the poor in the humble cot,
  As well as the halls of kings.

He soothes the sailor-boy to rest,
  And lulls the soldier's pain;
O, where on earth can a spot be found
  Not a part of his domain?

In the silent gloom of the mid-night hour,
  His standard is unfurled;
With his misty crown he reigns supreme
  This monarch of the world.

—*Julia Bowring Maltese.*

Source: *Songs and Flowers of the Wasatch*, ed. Emmeline B. Wells (Salt Lake City: George Q. Cannon, 1893), 32.

# Eaten by the Lion of Time

# from "One Year"

*Margaret Rampton Munk*

## I. *The Beginning*

Such things ought not to happen
In the spring.

The white azaleas bloomed
In honor of my going,
And I left them knowing
They and I would be alike depleted
At my coming home.

Tomorrow marks a stepping down
From prayer to resignation;
The final period
To hope.

## II. *The News*

The scene was written
In advance,
Rehearsed as often
As the days of waiting
Would allow.

The curtains of sedation
Would be parted to reveal
My husband's face,
The good news broadcast
From his eyes,

Voice buoyant with the word,
Among the loveliest bequeathed
By Roman tongue to Saxon—
*Benign:*
> Of a kind disposition;
> Manifesting gentleness and mildness;
> Tending to promote well-being;
> Beneficial.

And I would bathe
The hard, brusque pillow
With some grateful tears,
Burrow into healing sleep,
And wake to life resumed.

Instead,
Along the timeless, lightless hours
Spanning days and nights indifferently,
The sluggish curtain lifted,
Hesitated,
Fell,
And lurched again,
Three times allowing glimpses
Of a vision so unwelcome
That narcosis masqueraded ably
As a fair seducer,
Come to lure me back.

The face was right,
The eyes were there,
The voice.
The word was wrong.

*Malignant:*
>Showing great malevolence;
>Actively evil in nature;
>Threatening to life or health;
>Deadly.

The third time,
The drug had lost its power
To be kind.
I knew.
Each morning I would wake
And know again,
And mornings would become a year
In which this once familiar body,
Turned traitor
Only halfway through the course,
Would be a battleground.

The cue was wrong for tears.
They waited, prisoners behind
A hard tube filling up
The passageway of sound.
So pain became
The gaoler of grief,
And I lay silently,
Rewriting.

IV. *The Nurses*

I will forget their names,
But not the kind brown hands
Applying dignity
Along with soap and lotion;
The quiet voices of experience,
Soothing shock and terror
With the balm perspective;
The shoulder into which at last,
The night I saw the truth
Inscribed on paper
In the correspondence
Of consoling friends,
I unleashed ten days' hoard
Of tears.

Never mattered less
The color of the hands,
The accent of the voice.
Never had I learned
From solemn ceremony,
Quilting bees,
Or angry feminist crusades
What helplessness and pain
Taught me of sisterhood.

## V. *The Hair* 🌿

I always had some,
Even in my youngest picture.
After it had darkened,
My parents told me how
They once could hide a penny
Of new copper there
Among the strands.

It grew prolifically haphazard
Down a shy and conscientious
Schoolchild's back,
And hung below my waist
In auburn ropes
Plaited during every breakfast
By my mother's fingers.
Once,
I purposely released the bands
And let the waves fall free
Until the teacher
Bound them back.

At Easter,
Armed with cotton rags,
Like a determined healer
Binding up some annual wound,
My mother operated on a kitchen stool
Until it hung in shampooed corkscrews,
Ribboned to accentuate
The spring's new dress.

At eleven,
Sharp pain on the right became
Three days of tossing
In a hard hospital bed,
While woven braids dissolved into
A tangled nest I knew to be
Beyond redemption.
A kind nurse found me crying.
Did it hurt so much?
When I confessed
The honest cause of tears,
She sat an hour beside me
With a brush,
And not the scissors I had feared.

That summer
As a sacrifice
To junior high,
I underwent a second surgery,
And had them severed
At the shoulders,
To appear three decades later
In a Christmas box
Sent by my mother
To my daughter.

When we met,
My husband called it red.
I grew it long again
For him.

Today I combed it,
Clipped and brittle and drug-dead,
Into a basket
In the bathroom
Of my mother's home.
And she who placed the penny,
Wrapped the rags,
Preserved the plaits,
Joined me in mourning.

VI. *The Interloper*

When my husband went to bed in summer,
It was with another woman.

I hardly envied her.
She was less
Than I had been in spring.
Lighter by ten pounds,
Thin and scarred and hollowed out,
Both outward crown
And inward parts
That marked her as a woman
Gone.

This time the doctor
Was a lawyer,
His only remedy
The loving instinct
Of a man two decades married.

His sudden ardor
For his strange new partner
Was transparent, but
Remarkably effective.

## X. *New England Country Graveyard on an Autumn Day*

How much is spoken
By grey stone
Where time and rain
Have left it still articulate.

Too often,
As I stroll and read
By mellow light
Of mid-October,
The message is
The brevity of life.

This one was someone's wife,
But only long enough
To bear her man one child,
And bring it that same day
To sleep beside her here.

This one,
Despite the promise
And the strivings of a boy,
Lived long enough to be a soldier—
Never quite a man.

This couple lie
With tiny, grass-bound slabs
Strung like a rosary
At the parental feet.
How much life was left
In hearts too often pierced
Before they followed to this place
The children
Whom they should have left behind?

*Poems by Mormon Women*

God, God!
Not yet!
Keep me longer
From the darkness of those beds.
And when the colors on these hills
Are gone, and green,
And gold again,
Let me be here to see
With open eyes
And well-loved people
Just a call away.

## XI. *Remission*

These luminous November days,
A bonus bought with suffering and prayer,
Linger on as if they were aware
Of winter grief their dear tenacity delays.

Recalled to scenes I feared forever gone,
I cry to every shining leaf, "Hold on! Hold on!"

# On Dying Young in April
### for Ellen

*Nancy Hanks Baird*

*One hundred dollars worth of tulips*
*buried in the fall,*
*a pittance thrown at death's rampage*
*cannot prevent this leaving.*

An Easter wind rattles the trees,
thins the pallid sunlight,
cotton seeds collide randomly,
like one hundred peals of laughter.
The earth shudders, opens its clenched fingers
raises up the burning tulips.

If I could take your tired face in my hands,
whisper to the confusion in your eyes,
I would tell you, softer than the April wind,
more gentle than the cotton,
the secret for living and dying
is in the children.

Timid, bawdy, brave as the
first day of Spring,
sturdy as tulips, abandoned as the cotton,
sober and wise as angels,
they wake and sleep in wholeness.

If I could put my child in your arms,
lay her cheek against your breast,
pat your throat with her healing hand,
she could not cure what the disease has stolen,
but she would heal with her purity
the wounds.

So when earth wraps you in gentle arms,
lays you tenderly down in the tulips,
look for the children, menders of the breach.
Go in joy and wholeness
with the children.

# I Will One Day Be a Widow, Love

*Penny Allen*

I will one day be a widow, love;
Statistics cast that solitary role.
A wind will catch your reaching boughs and shove,
Ripping entwined roots from our shared soil.
From sharpest winds I shelter in your lee
And drink the rain that slides from your cupped leaves,
Yet your trunk's strength is doubled beside me;
Your pollen turns eternal in my seeds.
Not like the twining ivy, borrowing height,
That heaps upon the ground with the tree's fall,
When your support is gone, I'll still use light
And sway with circling seedlings and grow tall.
I'll branch the gap and find the seasons sweet,
But miss you, miss you, never quite complete.

# Coming Apart Together 

*Mary Lythgoe Bradford*

We exchange in great detail the weather report
We describe our coming decay and dissolution
Your sight has considerably worsened in one eye
Your dentist is into your mouth for five hundred
Your little finger reacts unfavorably to the cold,
and a close friend only four years older died.

I allow as how I'm hiding out from my gynecologist
since he removed certain valuable organs
My neuritis is still making a grand tour
of my body. My skin, it seems,
is deteriorating, my hair congealing,
and a childhood sweetheart died only last month.

And yet, we fall upon each other
in springtime lust just as if we still had
all our teeth, hair, eyesight, and internal organs
just as if we had been created brand new this year
just as if we ourselves had invented
the weather, our bodies, and love itself.

# The Shell in Silk 🦋

*Nancy Hanks Baird*

My father, whitening,
leached of rage and spear of justice,
now leans to my mother.
In his terribly,
exquisitely earned wisdom
even he does not see why he
sheathes his sword,
circles to her light.

Like an alabaster moth,
young and delicately flawed,
she floats by his side,
straining his sorrow,
curving her wings to hear him say
she is beautiful.

In their house above the black cliffs
he rubs her beautiful legs.
Bougainvillea filters the light, the room
in an aubergine wash.
Outside the screens, above the wet grasses,
spirit and rain are sheeting the mango trees.

She is everything he could never desire
or hope for,
a gift in an unopened silk envelope
left on the pillow,
a secret carved in the grain
of the perfectly turned koa bowl
gleaming in the rose and yellow light
of the quiet room.

# Full Circle Summer ❧

*Dawn Baker Brimley*

Fruit falls hot to the ground, alive.
That tree lives lavishly, for all of us,

has stood long in the sun, solitary,
for the proud August hours now gone.

One branch, bent with bearing,
leans on the aluminum ladder,

reflecting itself thickly orange,
heavy as guilt, ready to fall.

This tree seethes with sun, is wild
with light, awaits a kind of harvest.

Mother, it could be time for you to come,
to gather all that grows and waits.

If you bring a basket, make it deep;
and be unaware of any last chill in the air.

Some trees need hands like yours: calm
as roots, quick as the cracked stem.

I had not thought how I am spent
and parched; how I, too, look for you.

I had not remembered the heaviness of autumn,
or how much your harvest gathers me in.

# Invocation.

Oh my Father, thou that dwellest
  In the high and glorious place!
When shall I regain thy presence,
  And again behold thy face?
In thy holy habitation,
  Did my spirit once reside;
In my first primeval childhood
  Was I nurtured near thy side?

For a wise and glorious purpose
  Thou hast placed me here on earth,
And withheld the recollection
  Of my former friends and birth;
Yet ofttimes a secret, something
  Whisper'd, "You're a stranger here;"
And I felt that I had wandered
  From a more exalted sphere.

I had learned to call thee Father,
  Through thy Spirit from on high;
But, until the key of knowledge
  Was restored, I knew not why.
In the Heavens are parents single?
  No; the thought makes reason stare!
Truth is reason; truth eternal
  Tells me I've a mother there.

When I leave this frail existence,
  When I lay this mortal by,
Father, Mother, may I meet you
  In your royal courts on high?
Then, at length, when I've completed
  All you sent me forth to do,
With your mutual approbation
  Let me come and dwell with you.

—Eliza R. Snow.

Source: *Songs and Flowers of the Wasatch*, ed. Emmeline B. Wells (Salt Lake City: George Q. Cannon, 1893), 1.

# Relinquishing

# Fading Family Portrait  ❧

*Sally T. Taylor*

Lifting her paper bones so she can lie
On thick pillows, you bring your mother's tray,
Thinking of the unanswered question—why?

She eats a bite or two, then turns to cry.
You draw the drapes against the failing day.
Lifting her paper bones so she can lie

Again supine, you set the dinner by
And smooth her hair. You ponder death's delay,
Thinking of the unanswered question. Why

Does she live, lingering when she wants to die?
You touch away her tears. What can you say?
Lifting her paper bones so she can lie

Straight and flat, you sit a moment more, sigh,
And let the ragged thoughts come as they may,
Thinking of the unanswered question. Why

Is it said that suffering can sanctify
The soul? You feel her consummate dismay,
Lifting her paper bones so she can lie
Thinking of the unanswered question—why?

# Relinquishing

*Karen Marguerite Moloney*

We didn't know how softly you would die,
Who might have bled at any orifice.
You simply loosed a final, shallow sigh.
Your cheek is chill, but dry beneath my kiss.

Already cold, the quiet body lies,
The ravage done, small protest to the sheet.
Beyond the window through November skies,
Sycamore leaves go drifting to the street.

The nurses in the hallway, speaking low,
Are waiting now, impatient to proceed.
The yellow leaves are noiseless as they go,
But fall so easily—and gather speed.

# Our Beloved Mother Zina D. H. Young 🌿

*Ruth May Fox*

Sleep, belov'd mother, sleep,
Rest thee a little while;
Then mount to the eternal skies,
And ope thine eyes in glad surprise;
And read on banners waving high,
"Behold the just shall never die."

Thy life was beautiful,
Replete with noble deeds,
Right royal shall thy welcome be,
Lo, all the harps are strung for thee
And marshalled is the heav'nly choir,
Whose strains the very Gods inspire.

Thou wert exalted here,
Of women the elect;
But yonder there awaits for thee,
A crown for thy fidelity,
A place upon our Lord's right hand,
A joy *we* cannot understand.

We miss thy cheering words,
In blessing on our heads,
Thy never-failing charity,
Thy marv'lous gift of prophecy,
And sacred tongues, thy faith sublime,
Thy perfect trust, all these were thine.

And yet, we cannot mourn,
We so rejoice in thee;
But we will strive by his good grace,
Again to see thy saintly face,
To tread the path which thou hast trod,
Yea, even to the throne of God.

# Without End

# Invocation, or the Eternal Father and Mother ❧

*Eliza R. Snow*

O my Father, thou that dwellest
In the high and glorious place,
When shall I regain thy presence,
And again behold thy face?
In thy holy habitation,
Did my spirit once reside?
In my first primeval childhood,
Was I nurtured near thy side?

For a wise and glorious purpose
Thou hast placed me here on earth,
And withheld the recollection
Of my former friends and birth.
Yet ofttimes a secret something
Whispered, "You're a stranger here."
And I felt that I had wandered
From a more exalted sphere.

I had learned to call thee Father,
Through thy Spirit from on high;
But until the key of knowledge
Was restored, I knew not why.
In the heavens are parents single?
No; the thought makes reason stare!
Truth is reason, truth eternal
Tells me I've a mother there.

When I leave this frail existence,
When I lay this mortal by,
Father, Mother, may I meet you
In your royal courts on high?
Then, at length, when I've completed
All you sent me forth to do,
With your mutual approbation
Let me come and dwell with you.

# Song of Creation

*Linda Sillitoe*

Who made the world, my child?
    Father made the rain
    silver and forever.
        Mother's hand
drew riverbeds and hollowed seas,
drew riverbeds and hollowed seas
    to bring the rain home.

Father bridled winds, my child,
    to keep the world new.
        Mother clashed
    fire free from stones
and breathed it strong and dancing,
and breathed it strong and dancing
    the color of her hair.

He armed the thunderclouds
    rolled out of heaven;
    Her fingers flickered
        hummingbirds
weaving the delicate white snow,
weaving the delicate white snow
    a waterfall of flowers.

And if you live long, my child,
    you'll see snow burst
        from thunderclouds
    and lightning in the snow;
listen to Mother and Father laughing,
listen to Mother and Father laughing
    behind the locked door.

# Authors' Biographies

## Nineteenth-Century Authors

### Sarah Carmichael (1838–1901)

Sarah Elizabeth Carmichael arrived in the Salt Lake Valley with her family in 1850. Her literary talent developed in the West with the support of her father and in spite of pioneer Utah's limited educational resources. The gifted young writer saw her first poem published in the *Deseret News* in 1858, a piece so well done some doubted its authorship. The Salt Lake City paper went on to print more than fifty of her poems over the next eight years. At age twenty, she received both encouragement and public praise from Eliza R. Snow. Sarah's appeal came from her ability to speak on themes such as friendship, personal integrity, and love from a nonsectarian stance. Often called a literary genius, she received national recognition when William Cullen Bryant and May Wentworth each selected her poems for their anthologies. In 1866 a group of her friends and admirers came together to publish a volume of twenty-six of her poems. That same year she married Jonathan M. Williamson, an army surgeon who had been stationed at Camp Douglas. Carmichael's literary zenith was cut short when a year after her marriage she suffered an unspecified mental decline that may have been the result of a genetic problem, her parents being "double cousins." She died in 1901 after more than thirty years of mental debilitation. See also Miriam B. Murphy, "Sarah Elizabeth Carmichael: Poetic Genius of Pioneer Utah," in *Worth Their Salt: Notable but Often Unnoted Women of Utah,* ed. Colleen Whitley (Logan: Utah State University Press, 1996), 61–74.

## Augusta Joyce Crocheron (1844–1915)

Augusta was nearly two years old when her convert parents, Caroline and John Joyce, sold all they owned and sailed from New York to California with Samuel Brannan's expedition in 1846. After an unbearable six-month voyage, the family arrived in what is now San Francisco only to find desolate living conditions in a land at war with Mexico. The 1849 gold rush brought prosperity to the area but also the alcohol that ruined John and, ultimately, the marriage. Caroline later remarried, and in 1867 the family settled permanently in Utah. In 1870, Augusta married George W. Crocheron as a plural wife and together they had three sons and two daughters. As a writer she expressed herself in both poetry and prose, contributing regularly to Mormon journals and winning awards for two of her short stories. In 1880 she accepted the advice and aid of friends such as Emmeline B. Wells and published her collection of verse, *Wild Flowers of Deseret.* Ten years later she penned a volume of moral stories and poems for children called *The Children's Book.* Church history enthusiasts may be most familiar with her collection of biographical sketches, *Representative Women of Deseret* (1884), an early attempt to recognize the contributions of Mormon women and a valuable resource for historians. See also Augusta Joyce Crocheron, comp., *Representative Women of Deseret* (Salt Lake City: J. C. Graham, 1884).

## Lu Dalton (1847–1925)

Lucinda Lee Dalton's family made the overland trek to Utah in 1849 and moved to San Bernardino, California, on a settling mission two years later. After seven years they returned to Utah, to the small community of Beaver. An intelligent and gifted daughter of a school teacher, she was often frustrated that the "mixed and ill-regulated schools of new countries" could not provide her with more than a scattered education. Her love of learning stayed with her, and she began training for her own career as a teacher at the tender age of twelve. In 1868 she became the fourth wife of Charles Wakeman Dalton and eventually gave birth to six children, two of whom died in infancy. The marriage turned out to be a difficult one at best, in part because of Charles's drinking. An ardent suffragist, Dalton believed that women and men must work as partners on equal footing for all to progress, and this thesis was central to her writing. From 1872 to 1900 her persuasive essays and insightful poems appeared regularly in the pages of *Woman's Exponent*, addressing such topics as the power of woman's traditional roles, her right to education, property, suffrage, custody of her children, and fair wages. Her works were included in the *Utah Woman Suffrage Song Book* as well as *Young Woman's Journal, Contributor,* and *Juvenile Instructor.* Selected poems saw national exposure when "The River" was included in *Songs and Flowers of the Wasatch,* a book of representative Mormon women's poetry and art assembled for the Columbian Exposition of 1893; and "Gleams of Light" and "Longing" appeared in the anthology *Local and National Poets of America* (1890). See also Sheree Maxwell Bench, "'Woman Arise!': Political Work in the Writings of Lu Dalton" (master's thesis, Brigham Young University, 2002).

## Nina Eckart (n.d.)

Nina Winslow Eckart is one of many late nineteenth-century women who left little public record of her life other than what appeared in *Woman's Exponent.* Research to this point has not located any biographical information; however, another of her poems, "Autumn Days," was published in *Improvement Era* in December 1898, and the entry indicates that at the time she was a resident of Salt Lake City.

## Ruth May Fox (1853–1958)

Ruth lost her mother when she was just a toddler in England. As a result, her father was compelled to leave her with various family members while he served as a traveling elder for the Church. After immigrating to America in 1865, the fun-loving and mischievous twelve-year-old girl did factory and domestic work for two years to
help earn money for the long trip to Utah. When her family was settled there, she went to work in the woolen mill where she operated heavy machinery designed for men, believing she should receive a man's wage for doing so. She married Jesse W. Fox in 1873, and, over time, they had twelve children. Lacking formal education in her youth, she took college and correspondence courses as an adult. She served in a variety of Church positions and was the Young Ladies' Mutual Improvement Association General President from 1929 to 1937. Her busy life did not prevent her from working energetically for woman suffrage as treasurer of the Utah Woman Suffrage Association and as a member of the Salt Lake County Republican Committee. A charter member of the Utah Woman's Press Club, she was elected its president in 1897. Fox's literary efforts include numerous poems published in *Young Woman's Journal* and *Improvement Era,* song lyrics, and a book of poetry, *May Blossoms* (1923). Her most familiar work is the Latter-day Saint hymn "Carry On." See also Linda Thatcher, ed., "'I Care Nothing for Politics': Ruth May Fox, Forgotten Suffragist," *Utah Historical Quarterly* 49 (Summer 1981): 239–53.

## Ellen Jakeman (1859–1937)

Ellen Lee Jakeman was born in Beaver, Utah, the daughter of John P. and Eliza Foscue Lee and the younger sister of another talented writer, Lu Dalton. She exhibited literary skill at an early age, and as an adult she worked as a journalist and a typesetter. In 1889 she assisted Susa Young Gates and Lucy B. Young in canvassing Utah Territory for subscriptions to a new publication entitled *Young Woman's Journal.* The premier issue included her article, "Spiritualism, or What Became of Murphy?" It was the first of many contributions from Ellen, including poetry and short stories. Her work also appeared in *Juvenile Instructor* and in *Relief Society Magazine* as well as in Provo and Salt Lake newspapers. A strong advocate of suffrage and equal pay for women, she became in 1896 the first female to be elected to the office of Utah County Treasurer. An excellent speaker, she received invitations throughout Utah County to relate her experiences traveling in California and Mexico. She married James Thomas Jakeman in 1878 and became the mother of three daughters and two sons. See also Edith Young Booth, "Ellen Lee Jakeman, Poetess," in vol. 1 of *Treasures of Pioneer History,* comp. Kate B. Carter, 6 vols. (Salt Lake City: Daughters of Utah Pioneers, 1952–57), 1:69.

## Lula Greene Richards (1849–1944)

Born in Kanesville, Iowa, during a cholera outbreak, Louisa Lula Greene Richards survived two nearly fatal accidents as a child and grew up to become the first woman journalist in Utah. Her family arrived in Salt Lake City in 1852, after Brigham Young ordered the evacuation of Kanesville and all Pottawattamie County, and they eventually settled in Cache County. At age eighteen, she and her sister Lissa opened a small school, but Louisa was frustrated by her impatience with the students and by her lack of formal education. It was her desire for learning that in 1869 took her back to school in Salt Lake City, and there her talent as a writer began to develop. Early poems she submitted to the *Salt Lake Herald* and the *Deseret News* under the name "Lula" were well-received. A great-niece of Brigham Young, she formed a close relationship with Eliza R. Snow and helped her bring about her second volume of poems by selling advance subscriptions to raise the funds needed for publication. Her personal initiative and skill with the pen caught the attention of Edward Sloan, editor of the *Herald,* and in 1872 he selected her to be the editor of a new newspaper, the *Woman's Exponent.* Unsure of her qualifications for such a position, she accepted only on the conditions that Snow approved and that Brigham Young made it an official Church calling. For the next five years her editorials argued for the right of women to vote, to obtain an equal education, and to choose their occupation. She also advocated the right of Mormon women to practice their religion freely. She retired from her position after the birth of her second daughter, but she con-tinued to write as her family grew. Her poems appeared in *Woman's Exponent, Improvement Era, Young Woman's Journal, Children's Friend, Relief Society Magazine,* and *Juvenile Instructor.* Her book of poetry, *Branches That Run Over the Wall,* was published in 1904. See also Carol Cornwall Madsen, "Louisa Lula Greene Richards: 'Remember the Women of Zion,'" in *Sister Saints,* ed. Vicky Burgess-Olson (Provo, UT: Brigham Young University Press, 1978), 433–53.

## Eliza R. Snow (1804–87)

As a leader of women, Eliza Roxcy Snow's influence was

unparalleled. She was present at the organization of the Nauvoo Female Relief Society on March 17, 1842, and as its first secretary carefully preserved and transported the organization's minutes across the plains to Utah. She instructed the women from these minutes when Brigham Young called her in 1867 to travel to individual wards and stakes to reestablish the society Churchwide. She led the Relief Society in enterprises such as grain storage, silk culture, medical training, home industry, and political activism. She chaired the governing board of Deseret Hospital and presided over women's temple ordinance work in Salt Lake City and St. George. Proclaimed "Zion's poetess" by the Prophet Joseph Smith, she left a legacy of nearly five hundred poems on historical, occasional, doctrinal, and sometimes personal themes. Eliza's gift for versifying became apparent as a schoolgirl when she surprised her teachers by submitting her assignments in rhyme. Beginning in 1825 her poems appeared in more than a dozen different publications, including the *Messenger and Advocate, The Wasp, Times and Seasons, Nauvoo Neighbor, Deseret News, Millennial Star, Juvenile Instructor, The Mormon,* and *Woman's Exponent.* Early work appeared under pen names such as Angerona, Narcissa, Tullia, and Ironica. Her first volume of poetry, *Poems, Religious, Historical and Political,* was published in 1856 with volume two following in 1877. A promise made in her patriarchal blessing that many songs that "were dictated by [her] pen" would be heard by future generations has seen fulfillment as Latter-day Saint hymnbooks from 1835 to the present have included her compositions. In a fitting tribute, the annual poetry contest sponsored by the Relief Society bears her name. See also Jill Mulvay Derr, "Form and Feeling in a Carefully Crafted Life: Eliza R. Snow's 'Poem of Poems,'" *Journal of Mormon History* 26 (Spring 2000): 1–39.

## Josephine Spencer (1861–1928)

A somewhat shy but highly imaginative child, Josephine enter-
tained her friends with plays and stories she created. She lived a
comfortable life with her family in the same neighborhood as
Emmeline B. Wells and was good friends with Wells's daughter
Annie. Another neighbor was the elderly poet Sarah
Carmichael, whose talent she admired from a distance and
whose fence she and Annie would peek through. October 1890
marked the beginning of Spencer's prolific writing career. By
summer 1893 she had published forty-three poems and five short
stories in Utah journals and had won prizes in 1894 for two
short stories and an article. *Songs and Flowers of the Wasatch*
included two of her poems, one of them being featured with
other fragments of verse by highly respected poets Eliza R.
Snow, Sarah Carmichael, Emmeline B. Wells, and Hannah T.
King. A single woman, she began writing for the *Deseret
Evening News,* where she turned a small society column into a
full-page overview of the world of women and eventually
became the paper's society editor. In 1895 she published a book
of short stories called *The Senator from Utah and Other Tales of
the Wasatch* in which she addressed labor issues, an unconven-
tional topic among Mormon writers of the period. From 1902
until her death in 1928 she published more than sixty poems
and seventy-two short stories. See also Kylie Nielson Turley,
"'Untrumpeted and Unseen': Josephine Spencer, Mormon
'Authoress,'" *Journal of Mormon History* 27 (Spring 2001):
127–64.

## Emmeline B. Wells (1828–1921)

The precocious young Emmeline was a well-educated child,
graduating from New Salem Academy at age fourteen. She joined

The Church of Jesus Christ of Latter-day Saints in 1842, and within two short years she married James Harris, moved from Massachusetts to Nauvoo, and gave birth to a son who survived only one month. Poverty stricken, James went to sea in search of work, but his letters home were intercepted by his mother. Believing she had been deserted, Emmeline became the plural wife of Newel K. Whitney and traveled with him and his family to Utah. Devastated by his death in 1850, she began teaching school to support herself and their two young daughters. In 1852 she married Daniel H. Wells as his seventh wife and bore him three daughters, but her financial stability was still not secure. Under the name Blanche Beechwood she began writing spirited essays on women's rights for *Woman's Exponent*. She assumed the editorship of the paper in 1877, and during her thirty-seven-year tenure she argued Mormon women's need for educational and vocational opportunities as well as for their right to practice polygamy. Her position allowed her to become a vital liaison between the Latter-day Saint community and national women's groups, and she represented Utah at national and international women's meetings, forming alliances with important suffrage leaders. Her Relief Society work included chairing the grain-saving committee from 1876 to 1880, serving more than twenty years as the general secretary and becoming its general president at age eighty-two. As a poet and short story writer she was often sentimental, writing on reminiscences of her Massachusetts home, family relationships, and matters of the spirit. Many of her pieces that had appeared over the years in *Woman's Exponent* were collected into one volume called *Musings and Memories* (1896). In 1912 her lifetime of contributions was recognized as she became the first Utah woman to receive an honorary degree from Brigham Young University. See also Patricia Rasmussen Eaton-Gadsby and Judith

Rasmussen Dushku, "Emmeline Blanche Woodward Wells: 'I Have Risen Triumphant,'" in *Sister Saints,* ed. Vicky Burgess-Olson (Provo, UT: Brigham Young University Press, 1978), 457–78.

## Emily Hill Woodmansee (1836–1906)

Emily was the youngest of eleven children and was fortunate to be educated as a child. Her cousin Miriam brought the twelve-year-old Emily and her family news of a new religion, and the two girls, accompanied by William Bowring and a young Edward Tullidge, walked the Wve miles to a neighboring village to attend a Sunday meeting of Latter-day Saints. Emily was converted, but her family's opposition compelled her to wait until she turned sixteen to be baptized. She and her sister Julia, who had also joined the Church, determined they would leave England to gather to Zion. The young women sailed with the James G. Willie Company, and Emily pulled their handcart across the country from Iowa until the ill-equipped and starving group met with a disastrous snowstorm on the frozen plains of Wyoming. They took shelter in Martin's Cove until they were miraculously rescued by Saints from Salt Lake City. Deserted by her first husband with whom she had one child, Emily married Joseph Woodmansee in 1864 and had eight children with him. The blessing she had received early on which promised that her writing would comfort thousands of hearts saw fulfillment in her poetry. Many of her pieces were published in *Woman's Exponent, Young Woman's Journal,* and *Improvement Era,* and she was awarded a gold medal for the Sunday School Jubilee Prize Poem in 1899. She is recognized as one of a handful of foundational Mormon writers by contemporary scholars who have anthologized her work. Her poem,

"As Sisters in Zion," was set to music in recent years by Janice Kapp Perry and is included in the current Latter-day Saint hymnal. See also Mary F. Kelly, "Emily Hill Woodmansee, Poetess," *Young Woman's Journal* 18 (February 1907): 49–55.

# Twentieth-Century Authors

### Penny Allen (1939–)

Latter-day Saints may associate Penny's name (Penelope Moody Allen) with the texts of hymns no. 143, "Let the Holy Spirit Guide," and no. 71, "With Songs of Praise" in the Church's hymnal. Penny was born and raised in California. She received her bachelor's from San Jose State and her master's from Brigham Young University. She met Gary Lee Allen while she was on the BYU faculty and in 1963 married him in the Manti Temple. As a stay-at-home mom in Bountiful, Utah, she reared a son and three daughters. Her last paid job was teaching English at the BYU Salt Lake Center. Penny's poems, articles, and song texts have been published in books of compiled poetry, the *Ensign* and *Friend* magazines, and in assorted music formats. Gary and Penny live in Centerville, Utah.

### Nancy Hanks Baird (1951–)

Nancy received a bachelor's degree from Brigham Young University. She is married to John K. Baird, who is president of the Puerto Rico San Juan Mission. They are the parents of five children. A freelance writer and editor and the owner of a small business, she published a collection of poetry, *The Shell in Silk*, in 1996. Her poems and essays have appeared in the *Southern Poetry Review, Comstock Review, BYU Studies, Dialogue,* and other journals. She loves to run, grow flowers, teach poetry workshops, and try to speak Spanish. Learning Spanish is the most difficult thing she has had to do lately.

### Elouise Bell (1935–)

Elouise taught English at Brigham Young University for more than thirty-five years. She served as composition coordinator and as associate dean of general and honors education, and she received the Karl G. Maeser Award for Distinguished Teaching. On various sabbaticals, she taught at the University of Arizona, the University of Massachusetts at Amherst, and Berzenyi College in Hungary. Beyond the walls of academe, she was active in church and civic affairs, serving on the Young Women General Board (1973–75) and on the Utah Arts Council. She took particular pleasure in touring the West with her one-woman play based on the life of Mormon pioneer midwife Patty Bartlett Sessions. She received the Utah Woman of Achievement Award from the Governor's Commission on Women and Families and an Honorary Life Member award from the Association for Mormon Letters. She wrote columns for three Utah newspapers and published two books, *Only When I Laugh* (1990) and *Madame Ridiculous and Lady Sublime* (2001). Now retired, she lives in South Carolina and continues to teach an occasional class as part of Coastal Carolina University's Lifelong Learning Program.

### Mary Lythgoe Bradford (1930–)

The former editor of *Dialogue: A Journal of Mormon Thought* (1978–83), Mary is the author of two books, *Leaving Home: Personal Essays* (which won the 1998 Association for Mormon Letters personal essay award) and *Lowell L. Bennion: Teacher,*

*Counselor, Humanitarian* (1995). She has also edited a collection of essays, *Mormon Women Speak* (1982), and written widely on the novelist Virginia Sorensen. Her University of Utah master's thesis was the first scholarly work by a Mormon on Virginia Sorensen. Her own essays, articles, and poetry have appeared in *Dialogue, Exponent II, BYU Studies, Utah Holiday, Deseret News,* and in many other books and journals. Mary was raised in Utah but spent the majority of her adult life in Arlington, Virginia, with her husband Charles Bradford and their three children.

## Dawn Baker Brimley (1932–)

Dawn was born in Monroe, Utah, and draws insight from her childhood experiences near the mountains and lakes of Utah. She spent every summer until the age of twenty living at Fish Lake, Utah. She is a graduate of Brigham Young University in sociology and psychology. She also has the equivalent of a major in English. A former BYU faculty member, she has taught children's literature there and elsewhere. She has won several awards for her poetry, including the first place in BYU Eisteddfod competition in lyric poetry and the *Ensign*'s Eliza R. Snow poetry competition and second place in the *BYU Studies* poetry contest. For four years she was on the Church's writing committee, working on Relief Society lessons. She has also written song lyrics, most notably "Thy Will and Work" with composer Newell Dayley. She is married to Dr. Vern Brimley and is the mother of three daughters, grandmother of ten, and great-grandmother of a great-granddaughter. She has published a book of poetry entitled *Waking Moments* (1989) and is working on another. One of her poems was accepted for the 2004 war and peace issue of *Dialogue*.

## Marilyn McMeen Brown (1938–)

Marilyn has published three poetry books, fourteen novels, a history of Provo, and two musical plays. As well as earning three university degrees (two from Brigham Young University and one from the University of Utah), Marilyn has won several awards, including the thousand-dollar first prize from the Utah Arts Council and the first Mayhew Award at BYU. She also won the first novel award of the Association for Mormon Letters, an organization for which she has also served as president (2000). As well as working with her husband, Bill, as co-founder of the Villa Playhouse in her hometown of Springville, Utah, she raised one child of her own and five step-children and now enjoys fourteen grandchildren. Her latest project is the novelization of Richard Dutcher's film *Brigham City.*

## Marilyn Bushman-Carlton (1945–)

Marilyn was born and raised in Lehi, Utah, where she met her husband, Blaine. They are the parents of five grown children, three children-in-law, and the grandparents of one. Well into adulthood, she received a bachelor's degree in English from the University of Utah. During college she took a poetry workshop and wrote her first poem. Marilyn's poetry has been published in many journals including the *Comstock Review, Iris, Earth's Daughters, Dialogue, BYU Studies, Sunstone,* and *Ellipsis.* She has two collections of poetry: *on keeping things small* (1995) and *Cheat Grass* (1999). A third collection is nearing completion. She was the Utah Poetry Society's Poet of the Year in 1999. She is the recipient of both a prize and a grant from the Utah Arts Council, and she teaches poetry to students of all ages through the arts council's Artist-in-Residence program. She has lived in Salt Lake City for more than three decades.

## Elaine Wright Christensen (1948–)

Elaine's first book, *At the Edges,* won the Utah State Poetry Society book award in 1990 and her second, *I Have Learned Five Things* (1996), won the National Federation of Poetry Societies' Stevens manuscript contest in 1995. Her poems have appeared in numerous journals, including the *Ensign, Weber Studies, Ellipsis, Dialogue, Petroglyph,* and *The Comstock Review,* where in fall 2000 she placed first in the Muriel Craft Bailey Memorial Award contest judged by Stephen Dobyns. She received a bachelor's degree in German and English from Utah State University. A mother of five and grandmother of five, she currently resides in Long Beach, California, where her husband is serving as mission president. They will return to their home in Sandy, Utah, when their mission is completed.

## Iris P. Corry (1917–)

Iris Parker Corry was born on December 18, 1917, to James Elbert Parker and Lucinda Snow Parker. She majored in journalism at Brigham Young University, graduating in 1941. Iris worked for the FBI, KSL broadcasting, and *Improvement Era.* She served for two years on the Young Women's General Board. Iris married Elwood J. Corry in 1956. One child was born to this union, Dr. E. J. Corry of Highland, Utah. Iris has six step-children, whom she also helped raise, thirty-one grandchildren, and twenty-eight great-grandchildren. Elwood and Iris served a mission to San Jose, California, from 1979 to 1980. In 1987, Iris published a book of poetry, *Bread and Milk for Supper.* A widow since 1998, Iris lives in Cedar City, Utah.

## Susan Elizabeth Howe (1949–)

Susan, professor of English at Brigham Young University, is a contributing editor of *Tar River Poetry* and has just completed eleven years as the poetry editor of *Dialogue*. Her own poems have appeared in such journals as *The New Yorker, Poetry, The Southern Review,* and *Prairie Schooner*. Her first collection of poetry, *Stone Spirits*, was published in 1997 and won the Charles Redd Center Publication Prize. It also received the Association for Mormon Letters award in poetry for 1998. She has just completed a second collection of poems with Florida poet Terri Witek, *To Lie with a Landscape* (forthcoming). Susan lives with her husband Cless Young and their three aging dogs in Ephraim, far enough away from the Wasatch Front to be a peaceful haven she can escape to when she's not teaching.

## Virginia Maughan Kammeyer (1925–99)

Virginia was born on February 25, 1925, in Cedar City, Utah. Her father was a college professor and her mother a poet and writer, and Virginia followed in their footsteps. She attended Utah State University and Brigham Young University, majoring in English. She taught high school English for two years before marrying Fred T. Kammeyer in 1948 and having six children. She was active in the National League of American Pen Women, the Daughters of Utah Pioneers, and the Relief Society. She began seriously writing poetry in the 1960s. Her light verse was published twelve months in a row in the *Improvement Era* (1967) and five months in a row in the *Ensign* (1972). She published a total of twenty-eight poems in Church magazines. She won the Relief Society poetry contest in 1970 with "Afterglow" and the all-Church poetry contest in 1983 with "Harvest." Along with many other poetry awards, she also won the all-Church short story contest in 1977. Two volumes of her light verse were published in her lifetime: *Saints Alive!* (1970), and *More Saints Alive!* (1979). Posthumous publications include *The Joy Book* (2001), a complete collection of her poetry and three short novels. Virginia died August 10, 1999, in Lynnwood, Washington.

## Jean Gordon Lauper (1904–77)

Born in Canada, Jean Lauper spent most of her life in San Francisco as the wife of Serge J. Lauper and the mother of four daughters. She had many fans and admirers because of her charm, her enthusiasm for life, and her witty ways. She possessed great skill as a choral conductor and demonstrated administrative mastery in organizing a broad range of cultural activities in religious and civic groups. Her deft ways were demonstrated in her sewing skills and her genealogy work. She tossed off only a few clever poems in her time and would be surprised and pleased to find herself set to music by her granddaughter-in-law Harriet Petherick Bushman.

## Karen Marguerite Moloney (1951–)

Karen Marguerite Moloney, professor of English at Weber State University, earned a PhD in Modern British and Anglo-Irish literature at University of California at Los Angeles and wrote a poetry thesis for her creative writing master's thesis at Brigham Young University. She has published literary criticism (on Irish writers and postcolonialism), essays, reviews, and poetry in *Twentieth Century Literature, The Jacaranda Review, Dialogue, Sunstone, Weber Studies, BYU Studies, Exponent II,* the *Ensign, Westwind, Wye,* and several essay collections. Her hymn lyrics appeared in the 1978–79 Young Women's Laurel manual, and her poems have been anthologized in *Harvest: Contemporary Mormon Poems* (1989). Her writing awards include the Fred Weld Herman Memorial Prize from the Academy of American Poets for "Relinquishing," the Carole Elzer Poetry Award, and first-place awards in the Mayhew and Mormon Arts poetry contests. She served as the editor of *Dialogue* for its special 2004 issue on war and peace.

## Margaret Rampton Munk (1941–86)

The daughter of Utah's three-term governor Calvin L. Rampton and Lucy Beth Cardon, Margaret "Meg" Rampton Munk grew up "in a family of Mormon pioneer ancestry." After graduating from the University of Utah, where she first began writing poetry, Meg went to Harvard for graduate work in political science. She met Russell Munk while working in Washington, D.C., following her freshman year of college, and they were later married while in graduate school.

Russ's work took them to Japan for two years and then to the Philippines for five. Meg taught political science classes at Jesuit universities in both Tokyo and Manila. While in the Philippines, the Munks adopted their children Laura and Dan, and Meg's focus became her family. Most of her poems dealt with her personal experiences, and several were published in *Exponent II*. After returning to the United States, the Munks adopted a third child, Andrew. In 1983, Meg was diagnosed with ovarian cancer. After undergoing surgery and a year of chemotherapy she wrote the poem sequence "One Year." The cancer proved fatal in 1986. Her collection of poetry, *So Far* (1986), was published just before her death.

## Carol Clark Ottesen (1930–)

Carol Clark Ottesen received a bachelor's in music from Brigham Young University and a master's from California State University at Dominguez Hills. She also did graduate work at Claremont Graduate School. She is a former writing instructor at California State University, Los Angeles Harbor College, and BYU. For two years she and her husband taught English at Shandong Medical University and then at Peking University, People's Republic of China. She has a book of poetry, *Line upon Line* (1975), and a nonfiction book about teaching culturally diverse students. Her poems, stories, and essays have appeared in several publications. She and her husband have six children and live in Mapleton, Utah. For Christmas 2003 they went to Honduras on a humanitarian project.

## Dixie L. Partridge (1943–)

Dixie Lee Henderson Partridge grew up with seven siblings on a Wyoming farm homesteaded by her great-grandfather. Stories rooted in that childhood make up many of the poems of her two published books, *Deer in the Haystacks* (1984), and *Watermark* (1991), which received the national Eileen W. Barnes Award for a book of poetry
by a woman over forty. Dixie's poetry has won several awards and is widely published in national and regional journals and anthologies; she is working on two additional book manuscripts. Dixie earned a degree in English from Brigham Young University and studied in Northwest writing workshops. She has edited poetry for a River Writing anthology and currently serves as the poetry editor of two journals. She and her husband Jerry have raised their six children in Richland, Washington, near the Columbia River. Much of Dixie's work

carries a strong sense of place and history and a tone of emotional or spiritual change, displacement, or discovery.

## Carol Lynn Pearson (1939–)

Carol Lynn Pearson, who has a master's degree in theater from Brigham Young University, has been a professional writer, speaker, and performer for many years. Many of her poems have been reprinted in such places as Ann Landers' column and *Chicken Soup for the Soul,* as well as in college literary textbooks. The poems appear now in a compilation, *Picture Window* (1996). Her autobiography *Goodbye, I Love You* (1986) tells the story of her marriage to a homosexual man, their divorce, ongoing friendship, and her caring for him as he died of AIDS. Carol Lynn has written numerous educational motion pictures, including the well-known *Cipher in the Snow* (1973), as well as many plays and musicals, two of which were commissioned by Sundance Theater. She both wrote and acted in *Mother Wove the Morning* (1989). She has written seven inspirational books under the series title *Fables for Our Times.* Her most recent book, *Consider the Butterfly: Transforming Your Life through Meaningful Coincidence,* was a finalist in the Inspirational/Spiritual category of the 2002 Independent Publishers Book Awards. She is the mother of four grown children and lives in Walnut Creek, California, where she recently spearheaded a project called "Voices to Afghanistan" to help teach English to Afghani schoolchildren.

## Linda Sillitoe (1948–)

A University of Utah graduate, Linda Sillitoe has worked as a journalist for the *Deseret News, Utah Holiday* magazine, and the *New York Times.* She has won awards from the Utah chapter of the Society of Professional Journalists and the Associated Press as well as three nominations for a Pulitzer Prize for her stories about life in Salt Lake County. She has written three important books on aspects of Utah history: *Banking on the Hemingways: Three Generations of Banking in Utah and Idaho* (1992); *Salamander: The Story of the Mormon Forgery Murders* (1988, co-authored with Allan Roberts); and *Friendly Fire: The ACLU in Utah* (1996). She wrote the official centennial history of Salt Lake County, which was published in a popular format as *Welcoming the World: A History of Salt Lake County* (1996). She also has published a collection of poems (*Crazy for Living*, 1993), a short story collection (*Windows on the Sea*, 1989), and two novels (*Sideways to the Sun*, 1998, and *Secrets Keep*, 1995). Her creative works have won multiple awards from the Association for Mormon Letters. She has co-produced a PBS-affiliated documentary, *Native and American* (1993), and taught classes in journalism and writing on several college campuses. She currently works as public outreach coordinator of Weber State University's Stewart Library.

## May Swenson (1913–89)

The oldest of ten children, May Swenson was born in Logan, Utah, to Mormon immigrants from Sweden. She had already decided to be a poet by the time she entered Utah State University, where her father was a professor. After graduating from college, she went to New York City during the height of the Great Depression and lived in extreme poverty so she could have the best opportunity to learn to write and publish poetry. For the next thirteen years, she published only in small magazines and journals, finally receiving acceptances from the *Saturday Review of Literature, New Directions,* and eventually

*The New Yorker.* One of her poetry collections was chosen by W. H. Auden as a finalist for the Yale Younger Poets publication prize, but it was the fourth collection she put together, *Another Animal,* that was finally accepted for publication in 1953 by Scribner's. From this difficult beginning, she went on to become known as one of the most original American poets of the twentieth century. Among her many awards were grants and fellowships from the Guggenheim Foundation, the National Institute of Arts and Letters, the Academy of American Poets, and the National Endowment for the Arts. Her most prestigious awards were Yale University's Bolingen Prize and a $375,000 MacArthur Foundation fellowship. During her life she published eleven poetry collections; another five have been published since her death on December 4, 1989. See also R. R. Knudson and Suzzanne Bigelow, *May Swenson: A Poet's Life in Photos* (Logan: Utah State University Press, 1996).

## Sally T. Taylor (1938–)

Sally Taylor is professor of English at Brigham Young University. She received her PhD from the University of Utah in 1975, specializing in Shakespeare. She has published textbooks and a book of poetry as well as individual poems in many journals. She and her husband David served a full-time proselyting mission to French Guiana in South America in 1993–94. She is a shift coordinator at the Mt. Timpanogos Temple. Her community service includes Parent Teacher Association president. She has four children and eleven grandchildren.

## Emma Lou Thayne (1924–)

Emma Lou Thayne has written thirteen books of poetry, fiction, essays, and travel stories. She has been widely anthologized and has published internationally on kinship and peace among people and nations. She has been active in encouraging public attention to mental health, spirituality, and the advancement of women. Her words to the hymn "Where Can I Turn for Peace?" have been translated into dozens of languages as has her chatbook of poems about war and the environment, *How Much for the Earth?* (1983). She has been married to Mel Thayne for fifty-three years, has five daughters and sons-in-law, nineteen grandchildren, and two great-grandchildren. Emma Lou taught English and was the women's tennis coach at the University of Utah, where she was awarded an Honorary Doctor of Humane Letters in 2000. The Emma Lou Thayne Community Service Center is a source of great joy as it provides students and faculty at Salt Lake Community College with broad opportunities to serve. Her forthcoming book is *The Place of Knowing, a Spiritual Autobiography.*

.

# Bibliography

Allen, Penny. "Blackberry." In Eugene England and Dennis Clark, eds., *Harvest: Contemporary Mormon Poems*, 124–25. Salt Lake City: Signature, 1989.

———. "I Will One Day Be a Widow, Love." In England and Clark, *Harvest*, 126.

Baird, Nancy Hanks. "On Dying Young in April." In *The Shell in Silk*, 55–56. Utah State Poetry Society. Salt Lake City: Publishers Press, 1996.

———. "The Shell in Silk." In *The Shell in Silk*, 48.

Bell, Elouise. "Psalm for a Saturday Night." In England and Clark, *Harvest*, 94.

Bradford, Mary Lythgoe. "Coming Apart Together." In England and Clark, *Harvest*, 62.

Brimley, Dawn Baker. "Full Circle Summer." In *Waking Moments*, 14. Provo, UT: Bushman, 1989.

———. "Not Far Behind." In *Waking Moments*, 31.

Brown, Marilyn McMeen. "Will you Remember?" In England and Clark, *Harvest*, 112.

Bushman-Carlton, Marilyn. "Alisa Leaves for Medical School." In *on keeping things small*, 41. Salt Lake City: Signature Books, 1995.

———. "Summer School, 1960." In *on keeping things small*, 9.

———. "Voluntary Poverty." In *on keeping things small*, 34.

Carmichael, Sarah. "April Flowers." In *Poems: A Brief Selection*, 7–8. San Francisco: Towne and Bacon, 1866.

Christensen, Elaine. "Newlyweds." In *I Have Learned Five Things,* 38. Deerfield, IL: Lake Shore, 1996.

Corry, Iris Parker. "Nellie Unthank." In England and Clark, *Harvest,* 26–27.

Crocheron, Augusta Joyce. "The Baby." In *Wild Flowers of Deseret: A Collection of Efforts in Verse,* 53–54. Salt Lake City: Juvenile Instructor Office, 1881.
———. "Betrothed." In *Wild Flowers of Deseret,* 179.
———. "Thoughts Within." In *Wild Flowers of Deseret,* 112–13.

Dalton, Lu. "Woman." *Woman's Exponent* 21 (15 January 1893): 107.
———. "Woman's Sphere." *Woman's Exponent* 2 (15 December 1873): 106.

Eckart, Nina. "A Mother's Prayer." *Woman's Exponent* 27 (1 April 1899): 123.

England, Eugene, and Dennis, Clark, eds., *Harvest: Contemporary Mormon Poems.* Salt Lake City: Signature Books, 1989.

Fox, Ruth May. "The Bachelor Maid." *Young Woman's Journal* 24 (May 1913): 307.
———. "Our Beloved Mother Zina D. H. Young." *Woman's Exponent* 30 (October 1901): 35.
———. "The Relief Society." *Young Woman's Journal* 26 (March 1915): 151.

Howe, Susan Elizabeth. "Of the Beginning." Unpublished manuscript, 2003.

Jakeman, Ellen. "Your Letter." *Young Woman's Journal* 3 (October 1891): 14.

Kammeyer, Virginia Maughan. "First Date." In *More Saints Alive!*, 38. Lynnwood, WA: Far West, 1979.
———. "Morning Prayer." In *Saints Alive!*, 64. Provo, UT: Trilogy Arts, 1970.
———. "To My Dear Children." In *More Saints Alive!*, 44.

Lauper, Jean. "The Debt." Unpublished manuscript, n.d. Jean V. Gordon Lauper Collection, L. Tom Perry Special Collections, Harold B. Lee Library, Brigham Young University, Provo, Utah.

Moloney, Karen Marguerite. "Relinquishing." In England and Clark, *Harvest*, 214.

Munk, Margaret Rampton. "For Dad and Mother." In *So Far*, 20–21. n.p.: St. Mary's Press, 1986.
———. from "One Year." In England and Clark, *Harvest*, 139–45.

Ottesen, Carol Clark. "The Kiss." In *Line upon Line*, 6. Salt Lake City: Bookcraft, 1975.

Partridge, Dixie Lee. "Learning to Quilt." In England and Clark, *Harvest*, 150.

Pearson, Carol Lynn. "Mother's Post Pledge." In *Picture Window: A Carol Lynn Pearson Collection*, 153. Carson City, NV: Gold Leaf Press, 1996.

[Richards], Lula [Greene]. "An Apology." *Young Woman's Journal* 2 (November 1890): 53–54.
———. "On My Fourteenth Birthday." *Young Woman's Journal* 1 (May 1890): 272.

Sillitoe, Linda. "A Lullaby in the New Year." In England and Clark, *Harvest,* 188.

———. "Song of Creation." In England and Clark, *Harvest,* 187.

Snow, Eliza R. "Invocation, or the Eternal Father and Mother." In *Poems, Religious, Historical, and Political,* 1:1–2. 2 vols. London: Latter-day Saints' Book Depot, 1856.

Spencer, Josephine. "Poetry." In *Songs and Flowers of the Wasatch,* ed. Emmeline B. Wells, 22. Salt Lake City: George Q. Cannon, 1893. In L. Tom Perry Special Collections, Harold B. Lee Library, Brigham Young University, Provo, Utah.

Swenson, May. "The Centaur." In *Nature: Poems Old and New,* 13–15. Boston: Houghton Mifflin, 1994.

Taylor, Sally T. "Embryo." In England and Clark, *Harvest,* 121.

———. "Fading Family Portrait." In England and Clark, *Harvest,* 122.

Thayne, Emma Lou. "Sunday School Picture." In *Until Another Day for Butterflies,* 60–63. Salt Lake City: Parliament Publishers, 1973.

———. "To a Daughter about to Become a Missionary." In England and Clark, *Harvest,* 43–44.

Wells, Emmeline B. "Shadow-Land." *Musings and Memories,* 2nd ed., 86–87. Salt Lake City: Deseret News, 1915.

Woodmansee, Emily Hill. "Let Us Have Peace." In *The Poetry of Emily Hill Woodmansee,* comp. Myrlon Bentley Abegg, 217. Orem, UT: M. B. Abegg, 1986. In L. Tom Perry Special Collections, Harold B. Lee Library, Brigham Young University, Provo, Utah.

———. "A Mother's Farewell." In *The Poetry of Emily Hill Woodmansee*, 265–66.

———. "What Are the Fathers About?" In *The Poetry of Emily Hill Woodmansee*, 484–85.

# Author Index

# Poem Index

# About the Editors

Susan Elizabeth Howe is a poet and an associate professor of English at Brigham Young University. She holds a BA from BYU, an MA from the University of Utah, and a PhD from the University of Denver. Susan's poems have appeared in such journals as *The New Yorker, Poetry,* and the *Southern Review.* She has been a contributing editor to *Tar River Poetry* since 1992 and just completed eleven years as the poetry editor of *Dialogue: A Journal of Mormon Thought.* Her first collection of poems, *Stone Spirits,* won the Charles Redd Center Publication Prize in 1997 and the Association for Mormon Letters Award in poetry. Also a playwright, her play *Burdens of Earth* has been produced twice at Brigham Young University. Susan is married to Cless T. Young and lives in Ephraim, Utah.

Sheree Maxwell Bench is a research historian at the Joseph Fielding Smith Institute for Latter-day Saint History at Brigham Young University. A member of the Smith Institute's Women's History Initiative team, she is currently editing the diaries of Emmeline B. Wells for publication. She also sits on the curriculum committee for the Women's Research Institute and periodically teaches the introduction to Women's Studies course. In 1992 she returned to BYU as a nontraditional student and earned both a BA and an MA in English. She and her husband, Michael, have four children and four grandchildren.